# The SAP Green Book
## Thrive After Go-Live

# The SAP Green Book
## Thrive After Go-Live

Michael Doane

# The SAP Green Book

This book was written by Michael Doane.

Published by Michael Doane

Printed in the United States.

ISBN: 978-1-57579-415-0

# CONTENTS

# Acknowledgements

Ever since the 1998 publication of the first version of The SAP Blue Book, I have had a rich network of consultants, industry analysts, SAP executives, client leaders, and journalists. I have attended countless SAP events, including eleven Sapphires, and taken part in dozens of webinars. Since 1996, I have provided varying versions of an SAP Executive Seminar, the foundation of which continues to be enriched by the input of many time-generous contacts. While at META Group, I had more than 400 one-hour teleconferences with clients of ERP (mostly SAP) and learned as much from my callers as they did from me.

Many people in this network have directly contributed to this book as noted earlier. With gratitude, I cite John Leffler and Jim Richardson of IBM's SAP practice, Mark Wilford of Accenture's SAP practice, former META Group colleagues Dane Anderson, Kip Martin, David Yockelson, Gene Alvarez, and Stan Lepeak, Donagh Herlihy of Wrigley, Michael Bovaird of Sophlogic, Brad Wolfe of Intelligence, Rob Westerveldt of TechTarget, Ray Wang of Forrester Research, Bruce Richardson and Jim Shepherd of AMR Research, Paul Scherer of IBM, Pat Gray of Intelligroup, Tim Silva of Kraft, Rob Doane, David Sanders, Tom Hickerson, John Ziegler, John Bailey, Scott Lutz (from J.D. Edwards to PeopleSoft to SAP) and from SAP: Michael Myers, Kay Tailor, Jack Childs, Stephen Hirsch, Shai Agassi, David Urffer, and Mike Cornely.

## Contact

Client/reader input is golden and I welcome your comments. You are invited to contact me at any time at michael@michaeldoane. com. Argue. Complain. Elaborate. Query. Contribute.

All contacts will remain non-disclosure.

# Preface

Since 1998, when *The SAP Blue Book, A Concise Business Guide to the World of SAP* first appeared, I have regularly been asked when I will put out my next book on SAP. My initial intent was to write this book in 2001. However, once I began my research into the best practices for post SAP Go-Live, I realized that the vast population of firms with SAP software were still very immature in terms of their deployment. As such, proven best practices had not entirely emerged.

While the Blue Book was written to demystify SAP for anyone who has a stake in its success, this book was written for firms that seek to get the most of out of their SAP investments through enlightened organizational structures and adherence to proven best practices.

In short, the Blue Book addresses an SAP wedding and this book addresses the SAP marriage.

I could not write this book with confidence in 2001 or 2002 or 2003 because SAP, most especially in North America, was still in a state of flux. While SAP software made great market inroads in Europe throughout the 1980's, it was a minor player in North America until the announcement of SAP R/3 in late 1992. When I began working in the SAP fields in 1995, there were very few firms that had completed successful implementations. The entirety of the industry was focused on how to rapidly and successfully implement. The predominant concern was the time and cost of implementing SAP and, unfortunately Total Cost of Ownership was viewed as the yardstick. This obsession with time and cost resulted in near complete negligence regarding the best practices for post-implementation. A large percentage of clients raced to go-live…and then fell off the cliff.

Over the past eight years, I have increasingly worked with firms in the post-implementation phases of SAP. When I started this research in 2001, I found that I was largely alone. The balance of thought leadership (books, white papers, Internet content) was devoted to acquiring and implementing SAP and there was scant mention of post-implementation planning. I wrote my first white paper on the subject in 2002 and was I amazed at the outpouring of e-mails and phone calls from far and wide asking for more. Quite suddenly I had direct access to a number of clients who could share their experiences and, best of all, lessons learned, many of which included the unfortunate effects of rushed implementation projects. The upshot at that time was participation in a 2002 SAPPHIRE keynote on the subject of SAP Centers of Excellence.

In the years since I have participated in formal best practices groups for large and medium sized firms. In addition to providing advisory and performing more than twenty presentations on centers of excellence, I have continued to work with Michael Connor of Meridian and others to gather ever more best practices, methods, and means for making SAP more of a driver and less of a burden for its clients.

This book is not intended to address technical or architectural SAP considerations except in passing. There is an increasing canon for such subjects available each month. Nor is this book intended to explore various aspects of SAP products such as NetWeaver, Business Objects, Governance, Risk and Compliance (GRC), Sustainability, or Enterprise Performance Management (EPM). In the quest for SAP excellence and better returns on your investments, your firm may be knee-deep in any or all of these aspects; this book should provide insight into creating and maintaining an organization that will "hold it all together."

It may be that your SAP applications are in a pristine condition. SAP has run its external assessments and given you its highest marks. Excellence in SAP is to be commended. But even with excellence attained at this level, it may be that:

- Business stakeholders do not have the business intelligence they need to help the business evolve and thrive

- End users only fulfill the tasks they have been taught

- Despite a rapidly changing business climate, you have too little flexibility to do more than tweak the business processes

- You collectively have no idea what effect your SAP has on the firm's bottom line.

If your SAP applications platform is merely a functional utility, you are doing a fine job of standing still. This book will hopefully enlighten you as to how your SAP applications can be the vehicle to continuously move your firm forward.

# Introduction

So your firm runs SAP business software.

Congratulations?

In order to help you respond intelligently to that one word question, we offer this book. Further on, we provide a simple maturity assessment that will help you to locate your organization somewhere between the poles of No Way and Way in regard to your congratulations.

Implementing SAP software, or any version of enterprise software, is never easy. You may have participated yourself or simply heard "war" stories from those who did. Such stories include the business process design battles ("that's not how we've always done it!"), end user anxieties ("I heard after that after Go-Live we will all be fired"), budget strains ("these hidden costs are killing us") and data migration headaches ("we have seventeen codes for the same stock item").

Changing from green screen legacy applications that worked in discrete silos to fully integrated horizontal business-process applications is painful. But it can also be rewarding. Down the line, of course.

SAP claims more than 80,000 clients worldwide. (Their definition of "client" is somewhat malleable; most SAP watchers presume 55,000 to 60,000). We have no data as to what grades that various among them would fall into in terms of getting the most out of their investment. An informal poll of a half dozen analysts and consultants I know suggests the following breakdown:

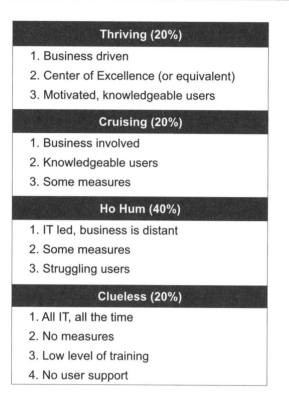

| Thriving (20%) |
| --- |
| 1. Business driven |
| 2. Center of Excellence (or equivalent) |
| 3. Motivated, knowledgeable users |

| Cruising (20%) |
| --- |
| 1. Business involved |
| 2. Knowledgeable users |
| 3. Some measures |

| Ho Hum (40%) |
| --- |
| 1. IT led, business is distant |
| 2. Some measures |
| 3. Struggling users |

| Clueless (20%) |
| --- |
| 1. All IT, all the time |
| 2. No measures |
| 3. Low level of training |
| 4. No user support |

Many of us in the consulting world have stories about those sixty percent of SAP clients who are Ho-Hum or Clueless. One of my favorites is the scion of a family-owned firm that took zero advice from his systems integrators, vastly under spent on the implementation and training, and then wished he'd spent the money on a new winter home in Florida (where end user training includes the positioning of lounge chairs and the mixing of mai tai's).

There are many potential reasons you have chosen to read this book. Here are some of the comments we have heard repeatedly over the years:

> "We implemented with one goal in mind, to Go-Live. As such we were totally unprepared to run SAP."

"We over-customized the software to avoid business process change. In essence, instead of getting a high-speed business railway, we configured SAP into the same business bicycle we already had."

"Since Go-Live, our firm is miles ahead of where it was but the business leaders keep asking us what return we got on the investment. Since we didn't measure, we can't say. We just know things are better."

"During the project, our business stakeholders worked with IT to make it happen. The day after Go-Live, they disappeared. Now IT is holding the SAP bag."

"The business processes are streamlined and the reporting is rich but no one knows how to use the software or act on the information."

Firms that adopt SAP tend to reveal to themselves "who they are." Revelations center upon how well (or badly) a firm navigates the organizational and cultural changes that an SAP implementation can engender. This extends to how decisions are made and communicated, how well leadership functions on both vertical (hierarchy) and horizontal (departmental) planes, and how vision translates into reality or into delusion.

One of the more interesting aspects of my fourteen years in this world is the fact that few individuals can ever adequately articulate why their firm is adopting or has adopted SAP. In dozens of instances in which I have provided SAP Executive Seminars, I have asked "Why are you adopting SAP?" and the response has nearly always been an uncomfortable silence followed by back and forth and sideways commentary. One such moment sums up the general experience and I wish I had a photograph as the client response to "Why?" was: a) the CEO looking at the b) CIO who has turned to the c) CFO who is looking at his shoes while d) everyone else is looking at the CEO.

Such lack of articulation extends into implementation projects and becomes ossified in collective organizational thinking thereafter. Moving off of disparate and interfaced applications running on varied data bases into an integrated environment is of course an excellent idea but such a motive does not play well across an employee population.

It may seem a cop-out but culture is at the heart of SAP success or failure. If your firm has strong leadership and embraces change, you will probably see benefit and enjoy a reduced level of operational problems. If your leadership is weak and you resist change, your SAP experience will be like an endlessly bad movie (as in just about anything directed by Michael Bay).

If your organizational culture is lacking, there is still hope as SAP can be deployed in ways that will actually improve that culture. Here is one example:

I once provided continuous advisory to a CIO whose insurance firm had recently implemented SAP. The CIO kept saying that she KNEW the business processes were much much better than before but that business leaders, lacking perspective, felt that the SAP acquisition had been a boondoggle. Needless to say, there were no measures of 'before SAP' and 'after SAP' so the argument was centered upon perceptions.

To counteract negative perceptions and to put the firm on the path of SAP satisfaction, we sought out an ambitious business leader and asked him to illustrate a business problem that SAP might help solve. We made sure to measure actual company performance relative to the business process in question. The process was redesigned and SAP was configured to enable the improvements. We then measured the results.

This ambitious executive had the enormous satisfaction of presenting to his colleagues how *he* had identified and solved a business problem and thus saved the company many thousands of dollars. This led to envy, of course, but envy of a positive nature as other business leaders stepped forth with proposals for other business improvements that could be enabled through SAP.

Inevitably, the firm created a Business Improvement Committee with the charter of saving the company money through the judicious deployment of SAP assets.

Result: a dramatic change in culture, keyed by a) an understanding of how SAP can best be deployed, b) constructive business and IT alignment and c) measurement. Note that, without measurement, the business leader would have had little to present to his colleagues other than what the CIO had previously possessed: "things are better."

Among the best practices of firms that have been successful with SAP are:

- Took ownership during the implementation: provided full-time talent to the implementation project and did not "leave it to the experts" to lead that project.

- Established "benefits-driven" culture and processes: exceeded the base measurement of time/cost adherence to assure that they actually extracted measurable benefit from the implementation.

- Adopted SAP best practices relative to processes (rather than insisting that they knew better)

- Maintained single instance/single version (or at least a viable limit of instances)

- Took a long-term approach to SAP (beyond implementation)

- Invested in organizational change management and continuous end user training

- Created a Center of Excellence (or equivalent) at the outset

- Energetically retired legacy systems (mastered Application Portfolio).

Going live with SAP is only the end of the beginning. Over the past nine years I have focused more on this subject than that of acquiring and implementing SAP software. In the course of my research and consulting experience, I have seen excellence at firms including Delta (my first model for a Center of Excellence), Wrigley (with a vibrant global Center of Excellence), L'Oreal, S.C. Johnson, and Texas Instruments (where best SAP practices are born). All have wrinkles, but so will Angelina Jolie.

I have also seen a major petroleum firm with nearly 300 instances on top of 300-plus JDE installations; a pharmaceuticals firm with seven separate sprawling SAP installations; another pharmaceuticals firm that spent $50M undoing $45M worth of ABAP customization just so they could upgrade; a wood products firm with six of twelve divisions on SAP and the other six in varying states of legacy hell; a services firm with 10% of its staff thriving on SAP and the other 90% stuck in manual labor; a small manufacturing firm with fifty users that ran through four project managers in less than a year; a global electronics firm that went live in more than twenty countries and then agreed that they had over-customized and so started the project all over again.

While I observed positive best practices at the former firms, I have observed other best practices at the latter firms as in, "don't do what they did." My concern, as evidenced in the preceding graphic, is that there are so very many such firms.

Note that I only mention a specific firm by name if I have observed excellence. The other firms will, for obvious reasons, remain nameless.

Time to thrive. I would love to name your firm in a future edition of this book.

CHAPTER 1

# SAP Marital Counseling

# SAP Marital Counseling

In my work as an industry analyst, I have found that there are a lot of sacred numbers tossed about for which I can seldom find a source. Eighty-twenty rules abound but why precisely 80-20 rather than 70-30 or 73-27? There was an old saw about how costs for enterprise applications were supposed to be in perfect pie chart thirds for software, services, and hardware but as we all know, a perfect third is a number with an infinite decimal 33.33333 and that the lesson of this pie chart is bunk.

In the late 90's, one of those sacred numbers was 3.2 as in "clients replace commercial applications, on average, every 3.2 years." While many 'sacred numbers' seem dubious, this one, based on my pre-SAP experience (from 1973 to 1995), that number seems about right. (As we all discovered during the Y2K studies, if you are in the Department of Defense or the public sector, that number might be closer to 23.6).

SAP clearly has a much longer life-span than 3.2 years. Back in 2001, I debated with a number of analyst colleagues as to the life-span of an SAP installation. My first bid of twenty-five years was met with general derision from analysts with mostly pre-SAP background. "No way. That's way too long." As it happens, the derision may have been deserved…in the other direction. There are hundreds of firms that have already marked twenty years or more with SAP. Thousands more will join them by 2016.

Despite this life-span, new SAP clients tend to think short-term, concentrating fully on the implementation project (the wedding) and giving short shrift to the long-term deployment (the marriage).

Many of the post Go-Live disappointments can be squarely laid at the doorstep of the implementation project in the vein of "bad wedding, worse marriage." Mark Dendinger, a fifteen-year SAP project veteran says, "There's a lot of needless pain out there."

Here is the classic SAP roadmap from maiden to wife:

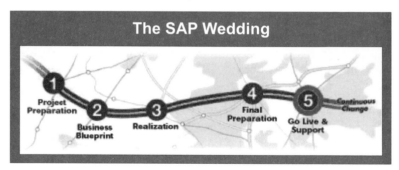

SAP weddings are often ruined at the outset from a lack of funding. Clients suffer from sticker shock and worse, will often use pre-SAP project costs as a benchmark. Thus, many projects start out late and over budget and are carried out with a collective sense of gritted teeth. In such projects, "getting it in" predominates at the cost of proper organizational change management, end user training, and other issues that are erroneously viewed as peripheral.

There are very few SAP divorces (i.e. firms dropping SAP in favor of other applications software). In fact, those that we have seen have been the result of a merger rather than a rip and replace. If for sunk cost alone, firms that adopt SAP are not at all inclined to drop it. The life span of your SAP will therefore be in the 20-30

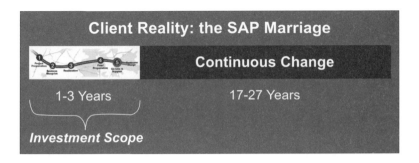

year range. If you implemented with little thought in that regard, you may well have set the stage for long-term headaches.

I have often debated methodology with leaders of the SAP systems integration firms. Across the board, their implementation methodologies include little to nothing in the way of long-term planning or post-implementation organizations. Their argument is often that clients are already suffering sticker shock relative to implementation and the addition of 3% to 5% more time and cost would be a hindrance to closing the deal. ("They'll find out down the line," remarked one morally upright partner at one of the Usual Suspects).

Faulty implementations can have a negative effect long after the Go-Live party hangovers have been cured. The table on the next page summarizes the most common issues faced after SAP Go-Live.

There are no simple solutions to the issues listed in this table. However, firms that move in the right direction will lessen the difficulties whereas firms that continue down the same path will merely aggravate them.

Some years ago, I wrote a brief article entitled "Shop Till You Drop at the ERP Mall." It was inspired by research, both primary and direct, into the ERP installed base (SAP, PeopleSoft, and Oracle). The research revealed that, after Go-Live, a large percentage of

## Implementation Issues Affecting Post-Implementation

| Issue | Long Term Effect | Solution |
|---|---|---|
| There was no quantifiable measurement of business benefits derived from implementation. | Business leadership has not seen "visible" value of SAP investments. | Value Engineering |
| We had insufficient knowledge transfer. | SAP support staff lacking competency and confidence. | Application Management Assistance or Outsourcing |
| After go-live, we broke up the implementation team and left IT to support the installation. | Business and IT alignment is lost. | SAP Center of Excellence |
| We shortchanged end user training due to time or budget limitations. | End users are lacking competency and confidence. | End User Training or SAP Center of Excellence |
| We over-customized the software rather than adopting inherent business practices. | Software maintenance remains an issue. Business staff cannot configure. | SAP Center of Excellence |
| We have too many versions or instances to manage, which equals not getting integration as planned. | Application maintenance is a burden and evolution is hindered. | Optimization or re-implementation |

firms tended to buy more applications software to the detriment of stabilizing their existing ERP platform through business process improvements, end user training, data synchronization, and the like. In short, rather than addressing the problems listed in the table above, they merely up the ante.

Software is not an answer to a business question. It is a variable in an algorithm that can lead to an answer. If you keep driving into a ditch with your fast car, getting an even faster car means only that you can drive faster into the same ditch. As Dane Anderson, an industry analyst and former consultant, reminds me, "The ditch always wins."

Therefore, let's turn our attention to good driving skills to change the outcomes.

| Issue | Long Term Effect | Solution |
|---|---|---|
| There was no quantifiable measurement of business benefits derived from implementation. | Business leadership has not seen "visible" value of SAP investments. | Value Engineering |

"Value engineering" is the fancy term for "working towards goals that have credible business numbers attached." This is the most common issue and it stems from a failure to view an SAP investment any differently from prior IT investments. Let's face it, before SAP most IT leaders could justify nearly any investment with some clever spreadsheet work, a number of bullets points, and the rallying cry of technical obsolescence. However, if your firm is building a new factory or buying out a competitor, you can bet the farm that a complete financial analysis will be prepared. The same should be done for an SAP investment but here is where the car tends to leave the road.

When confronted with a need to measure current performance, most clients respond with:

1. We don't have the time.

2. We already know things are going to be better, so why bother?

3. We can't agree on KPIs or we already have too many KPIs

4. It's not in the budget.

5. The project is already justified

6. We don't want to know (and/or do not want anyone to see who we really are).

Remember the insurance company CIO I mentioned earlier? Someone high up is going to ask the question: what did we get out of this investment? If the only answer you have is "upgraded technology," you have a fast creek, a downhill flow, and no paddle to speak of.

If in the course of your initial implementation you left the lion's share of SAP configuration to your systems integration partner, the result was certainly a lack of in-house SAP expertise needed to adequately support ongoing business change.

| Issue | Long Term Effect | Solution |
|---|---|---|
| We had insufficient knowledge transfer. | SAP support staff lacking competency and confidence. | Application Management Assistance or Outsourcing |

Your options to rectify this include a) further SAP training for your support staff, b) hiring in more experienced staff, or c) outsourcing some or all of your applications support. (For details, see Chapter 4, We Do It Themselves: Outsourcing SAP Applications Support).

| Issue | Long Term Effect | Solution |
|---|---|---|
| After go-live, we broke up the implementation team and left IT to support the installation. | Business and IT alignment is lost. | SAP Center of Excellence |

The alignment between business and IT is a sore subject nearly everywhere and firms that are implementing SAP are given a great pretext for getting the two together in a common cause.

For too many firms, this project partnership is ephemeral as the business stakeholders who participate in business blueprint are thereafter cast adrift and, once live, the SAP installation is solely in the hands of IT. This occurs even in firms that adopt the mantra that SAP is a continuous business endeavor and not a finite IT project. This subject will be addressed in various forms through the remainder of this book.

| Issue | Long Term Effect | Solution |
|---|---|---|
| We shortchanged end user training due to time or budget limitations. | End users are lacking competency and confidence. | End User Training or SAP Center of Excellence |

There is one solution that is by fair the most effective and also the rarest. Train your users. Not only prior to Go-Live but continually thereafter.

This "revelation" came to me back in 2002 when I was a speaker at a search SAP event in London. There were more than 300 attendees and I asked them to raise their hands if they'd had SAP for three or more years. Nearly all hands went up. I then asked them to keep their hands up if, in the past year, they had provided their end user base any formal refresher training. All hands went down. After a few seconds, everyone burst into embarrassed laughter.

The joke is on us.

On average, clients invest only 4% to 5% of their implementation budget on training of which about 50% is dedicated to the end users with the rest going to the internal project team and to executive awareness. Worse, since end user training is the penultimate step before Go-Live and both budgets and schedules are stretched thin, many clients cheap out and provide foreshortened training. Addressing a budget shortfall at the expense of subsequent user competence is a poor trade-off and is usually followed with a hopeful "they'll sort it all out" attitude.

The result is that users are hesitant, slow, unaware of their role in fulfilling a business process, and perhaps resentful. Since they are at the source of your SAP business process fulfillment, you will have undermined the entire investment.

Wise firms cultivate a culture in which the efficient deployment of SAP applications is constantly reviewed and refined. It is probable that your firm spent 5% or less of its implementation budget on end user training. It is equally probable that you have no formal budget whatsoever for ongoing training.

| Issue | Long Term Effect | Solution |
|---|---|---|
| We over-customized the software rather than adopting inherent business practices. | Software maintenance remains an issue. Business staff cannot configure. | SAP Center of Excellence |

For the sake of clarity, a reminder:

Configuring is the setting of business tables that determine the format, the nature, the location, and the destination of information.

Programming is the creation of codes that manipulate the format, the nature, the location, and the destination of information.

Programming, usually with the ABAP language, represents customization when applied to business applications. Configuration is relatively easy to maintain compared to customization. While high levels of customization are increasingly rare, some firms still suffer from customization that is based more upon "personal preference" than actual business requirements that cannot be satisfied through configuration.

| Issue | Long Term Effect | Solution |
|---|---|---|
| We have too many versions or instances to manage which equals not getting integration as planned. | Application maintenance is a burden and evolution is hindered. | Optimization or re-implementation |

This issue usually arises in undisciplined or poorly organized firms in which reporting lines, authorities, product lines, and/or regional considerations are in conflict.

No discrete action or project can overcome this issue. For the diligent, a long-term consolidation project can occur by which multiple instances are combined into a single instance. For example, a firm with ten disparate instances may consolidate five of them into one, another three into another, and end up with four. Reconciliation or integration across four instances is exponentially simpler than ten.

The large firms I have encountered with more than 200 SAP instances have no real solution other than to implement all over again.

———————————

None of the issues explored here are limited to just IT or just business stakeholders. All address both spouses of the SAP marriage which is why we are using the term "SAP marital counseling." Such counseling should not be characterized by the blame game.

John Ziegler, who was one of the first group of non-European consultants at SAP America and has as much field experience as any consultant in North America, is surprised when clients blame the software for implementation issues. "I have been involved with packaged software implementations for the past 20 years. In all that time, I have never experienced a business application software package that didn't work. That's not to say they have been 'bug free' but bugs get caught and fixed. SAP applications software has never been considered buggy. If it was, they wouldn't be in business today."

More clients blame their systems integrators than they do the software.

Mark Dendinger adds, "Clients are so anxious to get to go-live that it is often hard to engage them in conversation about what happens afterward. The best approach is to get them as educated as possible before an implementation project starts. The fallback is to get them educated in the course of the project."

So what about SAP in this regard? As a client, you have SAP software support, an SAP rep anxious to see you buy more software and upgrade regularly, and you may even tap SAP Consulting or some other systems integration partner for occasional assistance. As such, SAP is tangential to the long-term marriage/deployment and can be called upon for some level of marital counseling, especially in regard to technical issues, middleware, and training. Improvement in any or all of these areas will vastly improve your situation but will not solve it. Solutions are, finally, in your hands.

Whatever issues you are facing, one thing is certain: they are multiple and there is a lack of agreement amongst your various stakeholders as to what you should be doing to address them. More business intelligence? More applications software? Upgrade? Reduce customization? Train the users? In the next chapter, we address how to measure your needs.

# CHAPTER 2

# An SAP Maturity Model

❏ Denial, Realization, Determination

❏ An SAP Maturity Model

❏ Assessing Your SAP Maturity

❏ Best Practices for Evolving to a Mature Center of Excellence

❏ The Over-riding Importance of Business and IT Alignment

# An SAP Maturity Model

## Denial, Realization, Determination

Industry analyst firms such as Gartner Inc., Forrester Research, and IDC spend a lot of ink on maturity models regarding enterprise software, hardware, middleware, and the like. The concentration is upon the maturity (usability, robustness, flexibility) etcetera of such assets. At a given point, a product or service is deemed "mature" but I seldom see the other necessary arc in such a conclusion and that is the arc of client maturity.

SAP business software and its underlying technology have been generally deemed "mature" since about 2003. As stated earlier, however, we estimate that only one in five SAP clients is actually thriving. Needless to say, this observation leads to a belief that widespread *client SAP maturity* is not yet there.

After Go-Live, there remain a number of issues to be shaken out. The difficulty often lies in the prioritization of activities. Do you consolidate the gains you've made through the implementation of new applications? Push forward with extended applications? Refine end user competency?

As previously mentioned, much of my research in recent years has suggested that too many firms fall into the "Shop till you drop at the ERP mall" syndrome by which the purchase of more software is intended to address post-implementation issues. The result is that ever more shakeout issues are raised. The lesson is that applications software alone is not a solution but merely a possibility.

Another finding from that research is that SAP clients tend to follow a pattern of denial, realization, and determination in the first three years after Go-Live.

Denial is the presumption in the first year after Go-Live that all will be well once the installation is simply stabilized.

Realization occurs in the second year after Go-Live as the shake-out continues with no end in sight.

Determination to seek sounder solutions often takes place in the third year after Go-Live. It is at this point that a majority of clients understand that their SAP support organization is inadequate. The question thus turns to priorities and directions. What actions are required and in what order to improve SAP maturity?

## An SAP Maturity Model

The maturity model presented in this chapter addresses SAP in a complete sense, meaning an SAP installation that embraces most or all of a firm's key enterprise applications. The model will not work as well for firms that are merely using a small subset of SAP software (such as financials) in concert with legacy or "other" applications.

The model was initially developed in 2003 and has been applied at a vast number of firms. It serves to identify a client's maturity level and, even better, to provide a diagnostic to achieve a higher level of maturity. The underlying assumption is that greater SAP maturity will naturally lead to processing simplification, organizational flexibility, and measurable economies.

The model also points to the creation and maintenance of an organization that will sustain whatever maturity is achieved. We refer to this organization as a Center of Excellence. This term has been applied in a variety of ways and therefore requires some qualification.

First of all, you can name your organization whatever you like. One of the first efficient SAP organizations I studied was at Delta which dubbed its group the Client Care Center. The beauty of that term was that "client" meant not only passengers (full disclosure, I am a longstanding Delta Gold client) but also all of the Delta employees. Further, the term does not include that label "SAP." SAP is a means not an end and sticking those letters into the name of your business support and evolution center will undermine the task. Further, the organization should not be confused with what is often termed an SAP Competency Center. Most such centers are software-centric and are focused primarily on software and middleware performance. These issues are a subset of the subject at hand.

Other terms for such organizations include Competency Center, Business Improvement Center, and Business Fulfillment Center.

To avoid confusion, we will stick with Center of Excellence throughout this book.

In large enterprises, a fully functional Center of Excellence cannot be created in the course of a single project. Successful firms have built Centers of Excellence over a period of time. The best practice is to build this organization throughout the initial SAP implementation but very few firms have actually done so.

How to plan, build, and maintain a Center of Excellence is covered in a subsequent chapter.

The SAP Maturity Model is comprised of five levels of evolution, from the implementation of core applications through the establishment of an evolving Center of Excellence.

The focus is on four avenues of pursuit: business and IT alignment, enterprise applications, end users, and infrastructure.

Altogether, the model tests thirty-five best practices, each weighted for importance for each level of maturity. As a result, the activity categories are generally weighted as noted on the next page.

## Level 1 – Core Applications:

Clients may attain this level only if the core implementation and at least the majority of corresponding geographic rollouts have been completed, the end users have been satisfactorily trained, and no significant amount of continuing application implementation is occurring.

The client has agreed on a combination of processes, lines of business, and geographies to be frozen and hence supported by the Center of Excellence. Clients are advised to take a close look at the level of software customization that has been or is still occurring. High levels of customization will negatively impact their ability to move forward with subsequent upgrades of enterprise software or

| End Users | Business/IT Alignment | Infrastructure | Applications |
|:---:|:---:|:---:|:---:|
| 15% | 45% | 10% | 30% |

## SAP Maturity Model

| Level | Business/IT Alignment | Enterprise Applications | End Users | Infrastructure |
|---|---|---|---|---|
| 1 Core Applications | There is a link between business and IT for configuration updates. | Enterprise applications are not overly customized; core implementation is complete. | Basic end user training is complete. | Operational infrastructure is adequate. |
| 2 Stable Applications | The role of business in applications evolution is defined. | ERP is the backbone of enterprise applications. Interfacing is complete. | End users fulfill functions without excessive help desk or support. | Operational infrastructure is stable. |
| 3 CoE Defined | Business has active ownership of business processes. Current KPI is measured. | The applications portfolio is inventoried. | End users receive period refresher training. | Operational infrastructure is flexible. Applications data is generally synchronized. |
| 4 CoE Managed | KPI measures and targets are in the system. EPMO directs business process transformation. | The applications portfolio has been rationalized. | End users are trained to business processes and continuous training is in place. | Enterprise applications infrastructure is flexible. |
| 5 CoE Evolving | Business process change is guided by KPI performance; configuration is in the hands of business. | The applications portfolio has been optimized. | End user job performance is linked to business process performance. | Enterprise applications infrastructure is adaptive to applications changes. |

future enterprise software projects. For the first two maturity levels, SAP is the primary focus since SAP is at the center of the enterprise application portfolio.

### Level 2 – Stable Applications:

Applications stability is a combination of end users being functional, infrastructure being adequate, and the interfacing of enterprise applications to other related applications generally being in place. An application Center of Excellence cannot be adequately defined, staffed, and effective if enterprise operations remain unstable.

### Level 3 – Center of Excellence Defined:

This is the "hump" maturity level in which clients must turn the corner from simply operating the installed applications and move toward an evolutionary state in which the business and the IT groups are better aligned. Certainly, the definition of this alignment can happen much earlier — not only at the business process/data management levels, but also at the end-user level. Further, the client must, in this phase, begin to scroll together all enterprise applications, whether vendor-supplied or in-house/legacy.

We also recommend that the client engage in an application portfolio rationalization exercise. At this stage in the maturity model, a client must have key performance indicators (KPIs) established within systems, including a proper measurement of current actual KPI performance.

### Level 4 – Center of Excellence Managed:

A managed Center of Excellence presumes that end users are aware of their role within business processes. It also presumes that business staff members are actively involved in business process analysis and design, have direct roles in enterprise application configuration (where applicable), or have direct authorization over enterprise application software development. At this point in the maturity model, a balance will be struck between business-oriented staff and IT staff, in which IT professionals are guided by highly-focused business decision makers centered on business process improvement that will yield measurable business results.

### Level 5 – Center of Excellence Evolving:

An evolving Center of Excellence is immediately responsive to business threats or opportunities, with end users fully participating in business performance across business processes. Business processes are continually improved based on Key Performance Indicators (KPIs) and enterprise program management strategies. KPIs are benchmarked. The system indicates which transactions within business processes impact KPIs. Executive decisions to ameliorate KPIs are tracked in a knowledge management system.

### Elements of SAP Maturity

These include business/IT alignment, end-user competency, application maturity, and adaptive infrastructure. Without sufficient maturity in all these areas, clients will struggle to gain sufficient return on their enterprise application investments.

*Business/IT Alignment:* An IT organization is intended to drive business results and an effective application Center of Excellence; therefore, it must also be staffed by business personnel. Most firms fail to maintain this alignment due to a reliance on pre-ERP practices in which the IT group alone managed application evolution.

*Enterprise Applications:* The state of the applications (software, functionality, reliability, and interoperability) will have an impact on staff members' ability to impact change (business process improvement). Unstable applications will consume both IT and business resources with support tasks.

*End users:* These are the people who actually run the business processes delivered by the enterprise applications. Their level of competence, preferably driven by a continuous training program, will have a direct effect on business process performance and a firm's ability to absorb continuous change. Most firms have failed in this regard due to a reliance on end-user training practices that fail to address the extended life-span of enterprise applications and thus do not include continuous training.

*Infrastructure:* Enterprise applications can be stable only if the hardware/software infrastructural supports are in place. Software infrastructure includes areas like change management and testing (aka "Promote to Production") An evolving Center of Excellence will require a state of adaptive infrastructure by which changes to applications are reflected by relevant changes to the infrastructure.

Attaining a new level of maturity requires minimum performance achieved in the best practices for each level. As you will see further on, minimum acceptable performance is a seven on a scale of one to ten. Since the import of individual best practices will vary, we have assigned a relative weight to each.

These importance weightings have been used many times but it is obvious that each individual client will have different relative weights. The tool that I use in helping clients allows for changes to these weights provided, of course, that the total of all weights is 100%.

*Level 1: Core Enterprise Applications Implementation*

Formation of the Enterprise Applications Center of Excellence should commence as early as possible in the enterprise SAP life-cycle, but it will not mature unless all elements/practices at this level have been fully addressed.

**We are finished implementing/rolling out our core applications:** For this element, a firm must have completed its core applications implementations with all minimum interfacing requirements, and its business and IT resources should not be overly committed to ongoing geographic or organizational rollout. In essence, we seek to

| Best Practice | Weight | Category |
|---|---|---|
| We are finished implementing/rolling out our SAP. | 15% | Applications |
| Our end users have received SAP training. | 10% | End Users |
| We are not adding significant new modules or applications. | 20% | Applications |
| We did not over-customize our applications. | 15% | Applications |
| Our SAP infrastructure is adequate. | 20% | Infrastructure |
| Our IT staff has been adequately trained to SAP. | 15% | Applications |
| We have a link from business to IT for application updates. | 5% | Business/IT Alignment |

know to what degree the dust has settled over the implementation effort.

**Our end users have received adequate training:** End-user training is commonly shortchanged due to budget and time shortfalls. To achieve par for this element, the end-user community must have received sufficient training to enable it to run basic applications in support of business processes. End users should also be able to run reports, understand parameter choices, and build simple queries.

**We are not adding significant new modules or applications:** Any efforts to build a viable The Center of Excellence will be undermined if the installation suffers instability due to a lack of IT resources. Continuing geographic rollouts or application extensions will hinder a firm's ability to stabilize the application portfolio and thus delay center-of-excellence maturity.

**We did not over customize our applications:** If enterprise applications are heavily customized at the major business process level (e.g., orders to cash), IT staff will have a maintenance burden that will inhibit the eventual Center of Excellence when it comes to business process change (not to mention the upgrade difficulties in store since upgrades will not carry all customizations). This element should be scored in relation to both the number and the nature of the customizations made to a firm's software in lieu of standard software configuration.

**Our applications infrastructure is adequate:** Low scores should result if infrastructure is still vulnerable or lacking. Infrastructure can include middleware issues, networks, communications, and hardware that are affecting user performance (response time, accessibility, authorities, etc.).

**Our IT staff has been adequately trained to application support:** Normally, in the course of an enterprise application implementation, a part of the IT staff is trained in general application principles as well as software configuration. While most firms presume that configuration skills are the key, we consider it imperative for the IT staff to learn business process and integration skills as well. In essence, this element should be scored according to the level of knowledge acquisition made by the IT staff during and after the core implementation.

**We have a link between the business and the IT organization for application updates:** At an absolute minimum, there should be some communication mechanism between various business entities and the IT staff (or business/IT group) assigned to ongoing software configuration.

*Level 2: Stable Applications*

As Dane Anderson points out, "one man's stability is another man's chaos." For the purposes of this model, applications stability is a combination of end users being functional, infrastructure being adequate, and interfacing of enterprise applications to other related applications being generally in place. As you will see further on, we address the "subjectivity" issue by involving multiple assessment points of view.

**The SAP base is the backbone of our enterprise applications:** If there is no SAP backbone, maturity will suffer as these enterprise applications are at the center of the applications portfolio. Even a partial SAP suite including financials, order processing, and material management would suffice. If legacy software is the backbone of

| Best Practice | Weight | Category |
|---|---|---|
| SAP base is the backbone of our enterprise applications. | 12% | Applications |
| Our end users are functional. | 17% | End Users |
| We have sufficient IT resource to maintain stability. | 15% | Business/IT Alignment |
| SAP operations are reliable. | 15% | Applications |
| Business managers understand their SAP role/responsibility. | 10% | Business/IT Alignment |
| We do not foresee a major upgrade in less than 10 months. | 10% | Applications |
| Our SAP infrastructure is stable. | 9% | Infrastructure |
| Enterprise applications are generally interfaced. | 12% | Applications |

enterprise applications, subsequent steps in building a Center of Excellence will be compromised because software configuration skills for Center of Excellence members (rather than programming skills) will have minimum impact .

**Our end users are functional:** In a post-training mode, the end users are capable of fulfilling their SAP functions without overwhelming levels of help desk assistance. If more than 25% of help desk trouble tickets are training-related, this area needs attention.

**We have sufficient IT resources to maintain stability:** In essence, if a firm is constantly in fire-fighting mode, this score would be low. If, however, IT operations around SAP are generally routine, this should score as a seven or better. We note that firms in their first year of SAP operations tend to score low in this regard since the notion of "sufficient IT resources" is still in question.

**Application operations are reliable:** Business and end-user staff members will be primed for evolution only if existing operations are reliable. Reliability presumes a minimum acceptable percentage of uptime, a low level of software failures/bugs, and a sufficient flow of reporting such that the business is not negatively impacted by operations.

**Business management understands its role in applications:** Maturity will be limited if business management views the evolution of applications as merely an IT subject rather than a business performance enabler. However, if business management is aware of how the applications platform drives business processes related to business decisions, greater maturity will be achieved.

**We do not foresee a major upgrade in fewer than ten months:** If an upgrade of any key enterprise applications (ERP, CRM, SCM) is pending at this point in a firm's application maturity, it will be difficult to free up the resources required to build a Center of Excellence. It is possible that a major upgrade project will be combined with the creation of a Center of Excellence, which is the approach that many firms have taken.

**Our infrastructure is stable:** This element presumes that end users have the proper screens and printers, the servers are properly configured, the system has good availability and response time, and data security is adequate.

**Enterprise applications are generally interfaced:** Interfaces (both real-time and batch) between the SAP backbone and other key applications should be complete. The basic measure here is whether significant key interfacing has been completed to such a point that all business applications can operate efficiently.

John Ziegler says, "I visit a lot of clients who claim that their SAP is running pretty well but after gaining further insight I find that they have aimed too low. They can keep the SAP lights on but they aren't burning all that brightly."

## Level 3: Center of Excellence Defined

If a Center of Excellence is created in the course of an enterprise applications implementation, this level will be attained more quickly than otherwise.

Note that from this point forward, more than half of the remaining best practices (including four of the eight for this level) relate to business and IT alignment. Creating and maintaining such alignment is a major challenge as evidenced by the fact that every year of CIO Magazine's "State of the CIO" survey, it is listed as the highest priority.

| Best Practice | Weight | Category |
|---|---|---|
| We have business-assigned BP ownership. | 20% | Business/IT Alignment |
| End users receive periodic refresher training. | 12% | End Users |
| We have measures of our current KPIs. | 15% | Business/IT Alignment |
| We have inventoried our applications portfolio. | 10% | Applications |
| CoE organization is defined and staffed. | 20% | Business/IT Alignment |
| Senior. management sees a CoE as the means to improve results. | 16% | Business/IT Alignment |
| Our SAP infrastructure is stable. | 3% | Infrastructure |
| We have an acceptable level of data synchronization. | 4% | Applications |

**We have business-assigned business process ownership:** If a firm has established active business process ownership at the business level, this should be given a relatively high score. Active ownership presumes that the business people do more than request or approve changes to business processes and actually participate in business process re-engineering. In large organizations, such participation can be full-time.

**End users receive periodic refresher training:** By periodic, we are referring to quarterly or semiannual formal training events or, for individual users or a small group of users, a focused training session. In essence, the goal is to ensure that the end-user base keeps up with changes due to upgrades or business process evolution. This training should of course also be extended to new users.

**We have measures of our current KPIs (Key Performance Indicators):** This presumes that: 1) the KPIs that will be used to guide Center of Excellence efforts around business process improvement have been identified; and 2) current performance in that regard has been measured. Highest possible maturity would result if the firm has also determined industry and peer averages for the same KPIs.

**We have inventoried our application portfolio:** Inevitably, the Center of Excellence will embrace all enterprise applications. Thus, at minimum, a firm must have a complete inventory of all applications, including application name, function, interfaces, number of users, e applications to be included in the Center of Excellence. The end game of this inventory is the identification of all applications to be included in the Center of Excellence and, of great consequence, those destined for retirement.

**Center of Excellence organization, roles, communication channels, and charter are defined:** A complete blueprint of the Enterprise Applications Center of Excellence has been established and agreed upon by both business and IT entities, including the purpose/goals of the Center of Excellence, roles of each group, communication/ reporting channels, and (where applicable) budgets.

**Senior management sees a Center of Excellence as the means to improve results:** Senior management recognizes that the highest priority of the Center of Excellence is business process improvement (through which business performance, as reflected in the P&L, will be enhanced). Therefore, senior management has chartered the Center of Excellence to be a business performance driver and not just an IT management organization.

**Our SAP infrastructure is flexible:** As applications are stabilized, IT has demonstrated flexibility in providing necessary infrastructural changes on a timely basis without undue costs.

**We have an acceptable level of data synchronization:** Data synchronization across enterprise applications, whether packaged or legacy, is sufficient to provide flow-through of reporting and successful completion of key business processes.

*Level 4: Center of Excellence Managed*

In a later segment, I will address some of the impediments faced by firms attempting to maintain a workable Center of Excellence. This is the level at which those impediments tend to appear as an organization shifts to a direct business focus.

| Best Practice | Weight | Category |
|---|---|---|
| Business staff works directly with configuration staff. | 15% | Business/IT Alignment |
| End users are trained to business process roles. | 15% | End Users |
| EPMO directs major BP change priorities. | 15% | Business/IT Alignment |
| We have targeted measurable KPI improvement. | 20% | Business/IT Alignment |
| CoE organization is defined and staffed. | 15% | Business/IT Alignment |
| Our enterprise applications infrastructure is flexible. | 10% | Infrastructure |
| Our applications portfolio has been rationalized. | 10% | Applications |

**Business staff works directly with IT staff on configurations:** The business staff is fully involved in continuous business process improvement, and works in concert with IT staff to effect software configuration intended to reflect process improvements.

**End users are trained to business process roles:** End users understand not only system navigation, features, and functions necessary to fulfill their tasks, but also their individual roles in fulfilling business processes as well as the business benefits that are derived from successful business process completion.

**The enterprise program management office (EPMO) directs major business process change priorities:** The EPMO, via directives from senior leadership, collaborates with the business process owners, regarding major business process changes based on enterprise initiatives and opportunities.

**Measurable KPI improvements are targeted:** Improvements to key performance indicators are targeted (based on peer/industry comparisons and the firm's strategy), and the business processes affecting those KPIs are identified (online to decision-makers).

**KPI measurements are embedded in the system:** By whatever means (business intelligence, business warehouse, external control file, etc.), key performance indicators are embedded in the system and results are visible.

**The enterprise application infrastructure is flexible:** Since all enterprise applications are now included in the Center of Excellence, the IT group has demonstrated flexibility in providing cost-effective infrastructural changes across all business applications.

**The application portfolio has been rationalized:** Redundant and non-strategic applications have been retired and there is a clear vision for achieving a future state via the enterprise application portfolio. Just getting to this point is, for many firms, a massive undertaking since eliminating redundant applications can become a political nightmare.

*Level 5: Evolving Center of Excellence*

While I have found a number of excellent organizations in the course of my research and consulting, I have never seen a firm fully attain this level. That is simply a matter of "our reach exceeding our grasp." The stumbling points for even the most effective organizations tend to be a) ineffective business measurement and b) the linking of end user performance to business process performance.

**Business staff configures SAP/enterprise applications:** Based on business process redesign, an application management team comprised of primarily business staff does the following: a) designs non-customized changes to application software; b) provides functional specification to the custom application engineers; c)

| Best Practice | Weight | Category |
|---|---|---|
| Business staff configures SAP/enterprise applications. | 18% | Business/IT Alignment |
| End users are trained to business process roles. | 20% | End Users |
| Business process changes are directed by KPI results. | 20% | Business/IT Alignment |
| Business processes are continually reviewed and improved. | 20% | Business/IT Alignment |
| Our applications portfolio has been optimized. | 12% | Applications |
| We have a highly adaptive infrastructure for enterprise applications. | 10% | Infrastructure |

unit-tests software changes; d) ensures continuous updates to documentation and education to the end-user base.

**End-user performance is linked to business process performance:** At this stage, with end users already trained around one or more business processes, the client can monitor their performance not only in terms of the fulfillment of business functions, but also in terms of contribution to workflow and business process fulfillment. Ideally, such performance monitoring will be linked to career evaluation, bonus plans, and the like.

**Business process changes are directed by KPI results:** Key performance indicators are closely monitored by the business process owners. Results provide direction for continuing business process improvement than can be enabled through changes to the enterprise software configuration.

**Business processes are continually reviewed and improved:** The Center of Excellence reacts to business change/opportunity by reviewing and improving business processes on a regular basis, thus supporting continuous business improvement.

**The application portfolio has been optimized:** The enterprise application portfolio includes only non-redundant applications that can be managed by the Center of Excellence staff without undue complexity or challenges.

**We have a highly adaptive infrastructure for enterprise applications:** Infrastructural changes required by continuous business process changes are effected without undue delay, excessive internal burden, or excessive external costs.

## Assessing Your SAP Maturity

Assessments can be slippery business as they necessarily entail judgment. Who assesses what according to what criteria and with what underlying knowledge and experience?

Formal assessments tend to consist of a visit from the outside in the form of an analyst or consultant. With or without a clipboard, said consultant will question a number of stakeholders, sift through this input, and return with a verdict (otherwise known as recommendations).

Often the consultant will follow interview scripts. This refinement beats the pants off a general and meandering Q&A but organizational reality can often slip through the net of a standard query script as in "she didn't ask the right questions."

Shortly after I developed the SAP maturity model, I seized upon a simpler method that combines "script" with "organizational context." The method presumes what James Surowiecki terms "the wisdom of crowds." While one or two or three of your people will have a strong handle on "what is wrong" with your SAP, individual opinions will diverge and consensus may be elusive.

In this application of the wisdom of crowds, I advise polling a good cross section of business and IT stakeholders in regard to your adherence to the best practices included in the maturity model.

In the proprietary tool that I have been using since 2003, we usually have about twenty-five respondents who anonymously score their agreement or disagreement to their company's adherence to each best practice. The scoring scale runs from 10 (absolute and confirmed agreement) to 1 (absolute and confirmed disagreement).

Companies are not democracies so we provide a response weight to each respondent. Thus, in a field of 25 respondents, an individual with broad authority over business process design may have a response weight of 10% while a Basis administrator (with a lesser purview) will have a response weight of 2%.

We then score as follows:

Rating X response weight X best practice weight = result.

Any group result less than seven denotes a probable lack of maturity. Any group result less than six describes a problem. Any group result less than five suggests that you should heave something out the window (maybe your CIO?).

## Assessment: SAP Maturity Assessment

| | Stable SAP | Import Weight | Overall Result | |
|---|---|---|---|---|
| | Statement | | Result | Issue |
| 1 | SAP base is the backbone of our enterprise applications. | 12% | SAP is generally the base bone. | Yes |
| 2 | Our end users are functional. | 17% | End users need more SAP competence. | No |
| 3 | We have sufficient IT resource to maintain stability. | 15% | IT resource needs attention. | Yes |
| 4 | SAP operations are reliable. | 15% | SAP operations are satisfactory. | No |
| 5 | Business managers understand their SAP role/responsibility. | 10% | Management roles requires attention. | Yes |
| 6 | We do not foresee a major upgrade in less than 10 months. | 10% | Stability will not be affected by a major upgrade. | No |
| 7 | Our SAP infrastructure is stable. | 9% | Infrastructural stability is not an issue at all. | No |
| 8 | Enterprise applications are generally interfaced. | 12% | Interfaces are generally sufficient. | No |
| | | 100% | | |

| Category Result | | Overall Diagnostic | |
|---|---|---|---|
| Category | Diagnostic | Result | 6.92 |
| End Users | Energetically address shortfalls | Level Attainment | Shortfall |
| Business/IT Alignment | Energetically address shortfalls | Margin | -1.08 |
| Infrastructure | Strong SAP maturity element | Advise more effort to fully stabilize | |
| Applications | Nearly mature in this category | | |

It is a good practice to remove out the outlier respondents, those who are either too sunny-side up (all nines or tens) or too gloom and doom (all ones or twos).

On the previous page is a typical example of an assessment for level 2: Stable SAP

In the over-all result column, we provide words rather than simply the score. For example, the result that "SAP is generally the backbone" is based upon a score of 6.96. Where we find that the "management role requires attention," it is because the score is 5.85 which is less than the equivalent of "general agreement."

The diagnostic for this level of maturity is fairly clear as there are three results that beg attention:

- End users need more SAP competence

- IT resource requires attention

- Management role requires attention

The tool has other features, including an analysis of the difference in response between various groups (e.g. business vs. IT, one site vs. another, or management vs. line staff). We long ago noted, for example, that business respondents invariably assign lower scores than do IT respondents. The level of the response difference is a diagnostic of specific subjects of disagreement and how severe the level of disagreement.

General maturity (an overall score) is not entirely cogent. What matters is maturity by category of effort, as illustrated in the graph on the following page.

An assessment of this sort is not intended to be the final word in regard to your agenda. However, it provides a crucial "group consensus" bottom line in regard to the direction that an agenda should take.

| Assessment: SAP Maturity Assessment | | | | |
|---|---|---|---|---|
| **Center of Excellence Defined** | | Import Weight | **Group Analysis** | |
| Statement | | | IT | Business |
| | | | 45 % | 50% |
| 1 | We have business-assigned BP ownership. | 20% | Fair response alignment | |
| 2 | End users receive periodic refresher training. | 12% | Excellent response alignment | |
| 3 | We have measures of our current KPIs. | 15% | Group misalignment | |
| 4 | We have inventoried our application portfolio. | 10% | Sever misalignment | |
| 5 | CoE organization is defined and staffed. | 20% | Excellent response alignment | |
| 6 | Senior management sees a CoE as the means to improve results. | 16% | Slight misalignment | |
| 7 | Our SAP infrastructure is flexible. | 3% | Excellent response alignment | |
| 8 | We have an acceptable level of data synchronization. | 4% | Excellent response alignment | |
| | | 100% | | |

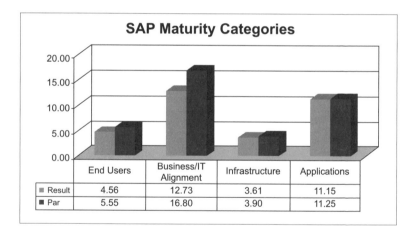

| SAP Maturity Categories | | | |
|---|---|---|---|
| | End Users | Business/IT Alignment | Infrastructure | Applications |
| Result | 4.56 | 12.73 | 3.61 | 11.15 |
| Par | 5.55 | 16.80 | 3.90 | 11.25 |

I was once a lead advisor to a branch of the Defense Department and I was concerned that my clients were lacking sufficient SAP knowledge to launch their very ambitious project. My recommendation was a two-day SAP seminar but they declined on the premise that they were up to speed. "We've met with systems integrators and other vendors and we've all read *The SAP Blue Book*. We're all set."

To test this premise, they agreed to an SAP Engagement Readiness Assessment that works in the same fashion as the maturity assessment described in this chapter. The levels of readiness tested are for the strategic profile, organizational profile, goals and measurements, consulting/education, and awareness and commitment. The results of this assessment were disappointing to the colonels which resulted in a major conference during which one man angrily stated "I don't give a god damn what Michael Doane says. I know we're ready!"

I reminded the audience that it wasn't I who was saying they weren't ready. "It's 75 of your own people, including most of you." They were convinced enough to invest some time and money to address the diagnostic. If it had been just been me telling them, and basing my opinion on a more traditional assessment, I doubt I could have won them over.

How formally or informally you assess your SAP maturity is of course entirely up to you. In that light, here are some observations based upon dozens of such assessments over the past five years.

- Very few firms have a handle on business measurement let alone business measurement at the key performance indicator level.

- Infrastructure, even when shaky, is a lesser impediment to maturity than any of the other categories of endeavor.

- Business/IT alignment is difficult to attain and even more difficult to maintain.

- End users always get the short end of the budget stick.

## Best Practices for Evolving to a Mature Center of Excellence

Clients that have already implemented enterprise applications and are seeking to improve Center of Excellence maturity should address the individual categories that need to be improved and seek to coordinate their relative progress.

Early in the maturity model (Levels 1 and 2), enterprise application issues predominate, while business and IT alignment issues come to the fore for Levels 3 through 5. Below, we take a cross-sectional view of maturity, and consider it from a variety of perspectives (e.g., end user, business process).

Clients are advised to address these categories as Center of Excellence-building activities rather than attempting to move in progressive fashion from level to level. Details regarding the "how to" of the practices are included in the upcoming chapter on Centers of Excellence.

### End-User Maturity

End-user maturity follows a simple arc from initial training to business process "ownership." Firms have been challenged to fulfill the remaining steps because of a lack of ownership/budget for continuous training and an inability to link end-user competency to business process performance.

| Level | End Users |
|-------|-----------|
| 1 | Our end users have received adequate training. |
| 2 | Our end users are functional. |
| 3 | End users receive periodic refresher training. |
| 4 | End users are trained to business process roles. |
| 5 | End-user performance is linked to business process performance. |

Levels 1, 2, and 3 should be directly addressed during initial user training.

## Business/IT Alignment

The stumbling block for most firms when it comes to business and IT alignment is the measurement and tracking of key performance indicators as business performance measurement is sought through other means or neglected altogether. Further, firms have shown a tendency to achieve a "to be" state and then cease to evolve. Maturity regarding business and alignment requires a continual refresh of the "to be" vision that should be provided by the Enterprise Program Management Office (EPMO) in conjunction with the business process owners.

If you do not have an EPMO or equivalent, you will need another means to generate, define, and pursue continually refreshed "to be" visions.

| Level | Business/IT Alignment |
|-------|----------------------|
| 1 | We have a link from the business to the IT group for application updates. |
| 2 | We have sufficient IT resources to maintain stability. |
| 2 | Business management understands its role in applications. |
| 3 | We have business-assigned business process ownership. |
| 3 | We have measures of our current KPIs. |
| 3 | CoE organization, roles, communication channels, and charter are defined. |
| 3 | Senior management sees a CoE as the means to improve results. |
| 4 | Business staff works directly with configuration staff. |
| 4 | EPMO directs major business process change priorities. |
| 4 | Measurable KPI improvements are targeted. |
| 4 | KPI measurements are embedded in the system. |
| 5 | Business staff configures ERP/enterprise applications. |
| 5 | Business process changes are directed by KPI results. |
| 5 | Business processes are continually reviewed and improved. |

## Enterprise Applications

A Center of Excellence cannot be established until the applications are stable and rationalized. This usually begins with SAP, which is at the center of the application portfolio.

| Level | Enterprise Applications |
|---|---|
| 1 | We are finished implementing/rolling out our applications. |
| 1 | We are not adding significant new modules or applications. |
| 1 | We did not over customize our applications. |
| 1 | Our IT staff has been adequately trained to applications. |
| 2 | SAP base is the backbone of our enterprise applications. |
| 2 | Application operations are reliable. |
| 2 | We do not foresee a major upgrade in less than 10 months. |
| 2 | Enterprise applications are generally interfaced. |
| 3 | We have inventoried our application portfolio. |
| 4 | The application portfolio has been rationalized. |
| 5 | The application portfolio has been optimized. |

## Infrastructure

Simply maintaining a stable infrastructure may prove difficult as the Center of Excellence reaches Level 4 (Center of Excellence managed) due to an increased velocity of business process change resulting from the enabling effects of vastly improved business and IT alignment.

Further, the maturity model defined in this document addresses primarily the business-centric aspects of an Enterprise Applications Center of Excellence. To arrive at full maturity in this regard, clients will necessarily move upward on a parallel maturity model for infrastructure and operations.

| Level | Infrastructure |
|---|---|
| 1 | Our infrastructure is adequate. |
| 2 | Our infrastructure is stable. |
| 3 | Our infrastructure is flexible. |
| 3 | We have an acceptable level of data synchronization. |
| 4 | The enterprise application infrastructure is flexible. |
| 5 | We have a highly adaptive infrastructure for enterprise applications. |

## The Over-riding Importance of Business and IT Alignment

Management of the SAP life-cycle is clearly not the realm of IT alone and most clients are required to significantly alter their point of view in order to grow more mature in this regard.

Throughout the maturation of a Center of Excellence, business and IT alignment rises in importance:

| Maturity Level | Best Practice | Related to Alignment | Percentage |
| --- | --- | --- | --- |
| 1: Core Implementation | 7 | 1 | 14% |
| 2: Stability | 8 | 2 | 25% |
| 3: CoE defined | 8 | 4 | 50% |
| 4: CoE Managed | 7 | 4 | 57% |
| 5: CoE Evolving | 6 | 3 | 50% |

Three barriers to this alignment are 1) business personnel do not want to be viewed as IT and 2) a chronic failure to measure the business benefits of IT and 3) the break-up of implementation teams after Go-Live.

To address the first barrier, be aware that language matters and IT is a business language-killer. Firms that successfully align business and IT tend to have organizations with neutral or business-centric monikers: Customer Care Center, Center of Excellence, Center for Advanced Business. Such organizations may have technical IT staff around, but the ambiance is strictly business.

The second barrier exists because many enterprise applications organizations are driven by a bullet-point vision that does not provide business focus. A failure to target and track business benefits during implementation usually leads to continuing failure to measure after Go-Live. If Key Performance Indicators are tracked, business staff will be more inclined to participate in a Center of Excellence.

In a great majority of enterprise application implementations, business people are brought into the team for a finite period, with a goal of completing business process design and configuration. Nearly all of the enterprise application implementation methodologies presume that this activity will occur once (as clients seek to move from As-Is to To-Be). Without a plan of continuous business improvement, clients revert to the pre-project mode in which business people request and negotiate IT changes rather than actively participate in those changes.

We strongly recommend that clients keep their teams largely intact, albeit at lower staff levels, after Go-Live.

Massive investments in enterprise applications are intended to result in even more massive business benefits. While most firms have shown some success in this area, few firms are taking full advantage of their enterprise application assets. While incremental improvements to any of the four key categories (stabilizing the applications, improving end-user competency, improving the infrastructure, and realigning the business with the IT organization) are welcome, only a concerted effort along all four axes will result in acceptable enterprise application maturity.

# CHAPTER 3

# Building and Sustaining a Center of Excellence

- ❏ New Life Cycle = New Dance Steps

- ❏ Pre-SAP Implementation Strategies and Best Practices

- ❏ Why Firms Need a Center of Excellence

- ❏ Center of Excellence Organization

- ❏ Transforming the "Build" Team into a Continuous Business Evolution Team

- ❏ Center of Excellence: Thumbnail Job Descriptions

- ❏ Variant Structures for Centers of Excellence

- ❏ Mastering the Business/IT Dynamic

- ❏ A Word about Solution Manager

- ❏ What Goes Wrong: How Centers of Excellence Become Centers of Mediocrity

# Building and Sustaining a Center of Excellence

## New Life Cycle = New Dance Steps

While the focus of this chapter is the management and maturation of SAP business applications through a continuous life-cycle, we will all the same include legacy applications, which will be defined as applications that were specifically developed for a client either in-house or through contractual application development and SAP applications such as Enterprise Resource Planning (ERP), Customer Relationship Management (CRM), Supply Chain Management (SCM, but often referred to by SAP as APO, for Advanced Planner and Optimizer).

Therefore, the Center of Excellence, if fully extended, should embrace all enterprise applications.

Since the first great wave of SAP software in the 1990's the necessity and complexity of managing an SAP life-cycle have continued to grow as both the breadth and depth of business functionality have risen exponentially. The vast majority of clients of SAP clients have interfaced these applications to retained legacy systems, thus complicating life-cycle management as these applications have differing life-cycles.

## The Legacy Applications Life-Cycle

Legacy applications are built and maintained through programming and have a higher degree of obsolescence than do package applications.

This applies to both fully custom-built applications and package applications that have been, through time, heavily customized to the point that they require programming maintenance similar to custom applications.

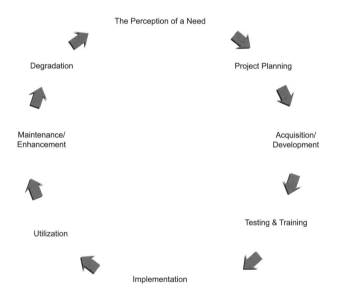

The cycle described above applies not only to the initial development of a custom application but also to subsequent application extensions, revisions, patches, and interfaces.

Application degradation occurs when the application no longer serves the business and/or the underlying technology of the application becomes obsolete. Vertical applications that are interfaced to other vertical applications tend to have a shorter life-span than do horizontal, business-process-based applications. For example, a custom-built sales order processing application that is interfaced to disparate accounting, procurement, and production planning applications has a higher probability of being replaced than a sales order processing application that is part of a suite that fulfills the Orders to Cash (OTC) business process.

Prior to the rise of software firms such as SAP, Oracle, PeopleSoft, J.D. Edwards, and Siebel in the 1990's, few software vendors were retained by clients for more than five years running, with the notable exceptions of American Software, Computer Associates, and SAS. The life-span of most business applications through the 1980's was between three and six years as technology shifts such as distributive processing and the increasing relevance of the personal computer led clients to rip and replace.

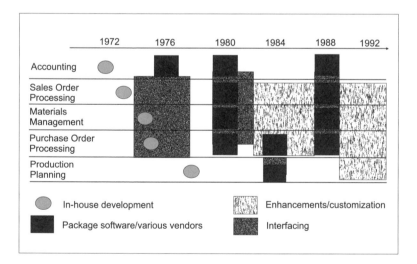

The Y2K debacle fueled this activity and drove many clients to ERP since in many cases the cost of such acquisition proved to be marginally more expensive than a Y2K fix.

## The SAP Applications Life-Cycle

Enterprise applications have long since proven to have a much longer life-span than legacy applications and this is the result of two key drivers:

1. Sunk cost: the investments made by clients when moving to enterprise applications software are of such import that abandonment after implementation is scarcely conceivable.

2. The critical mass, in terms of resource, revenues, and growth rate of major software vendors such as SAP and Oracle has led to a continuous stream of upgrades and application extensions, often negating the need for a client to enhance the software with in-house IT staff. This second point also leads to additional sunk cost.

As noted earlier, many companies have had SAP software for more than twenty-five years, having implemented R/2 in the 1980's, upgraded to R/3 in the 1990's and to newer versions since the onset of the new millennium. Thus, there is no "obsolete" point in the SAP life-cycle.

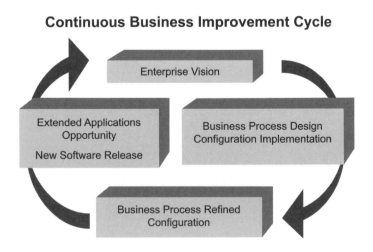

**Continuous Business Improvement Cycle**

Enterprise Vision

Extended Applications Opportunity

New Software Release

Business Process Design Configuration Implementation

Business Process Refined Configuration

In the following segments, we will explore the challenges and best practices for managing and maturing the SAP life-cycle for a client with core enterprise applications as well as a large number of legacy applications.

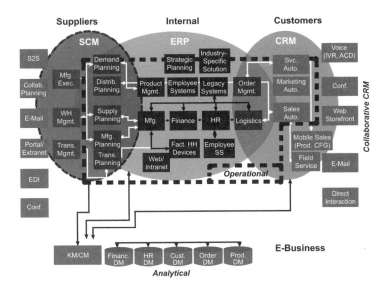

The applications portfolio is necessarily centered by ERP. Therefore, successful SAP life-cycle management will necessarily depend upon a high level of ERP integration.

## Pre-SAP Implementation Strategies and Best Practices

Clients move to enterprise applications for a variety of reasons but the two most over-riding benefits of enterprise applications are data integration and consolidation at all levels. The reduction of labor and of redundancy, the flexibility of process change, a high level of data integrity and ease of reporting can be derived if data integration and consolidation at all levels are achieved.

It is a fact, however, that a large percentage of enterprise applications clients fail to adequately achieve data integration and consolidation. What they have in common, beyond implementation mistakes, is a failure to view the move from legacy to enterprise applications with sufficient foreknowledge and strategy. In this section, we will cover the key strategic areas that must be addressed in a disciplined fashion.

### Data Migration/Manifest Planning

Enterprise applications implementation methodologies tend to include data migration and data manifest in a phase after blueprinting and software configuration. Given the import of this subject, we believe that planning of data migration and data manifest should occur even prior to software selection, most especially for large-scale enterprise applications endeavors.

Key master files for any enterprise applications installation are those for clients, suppliers, and materials. As clients migrate data from legacy systems to enterprise applications, two key obstacles arise:

1. multiple records for the same item, which require data cleansing

2. master records will not be complete as enterprise applications master files include considerably more information than do legacy master files, which leads to data manifest efforts.

The latter obstacle is especially important in that the tight integration of enterprise applications software requires that key master file fields be populated or functionality will not be possible.

As master file volume rises, these obstacles can become nightmarish and clearly the materials master is the most daunting.

Much of the data cleansing can be done through automated means but the effort required to migrate data from legacy to enterprise applications should not be underestimated. One Fortune 100 firm where we have experience estimated that the effort to successfully migrate 400,000 material master records from diverse legacy systems to SAP took five person years with the majority of this effort being given over to data manifest.

### Instance, Version, and Data Center Management Planning

Large-scale enterprise applications installations, with very large user bases, generally extend across multiple geographies, each of which is implemented at different times. There is no "big bang" large-scale implementation.

The long-term maintenance of common standards and coherent data can be jeopardized in three ways:

1. multiple instances or versions are implemented within the same overall installation

2. too many data centers are deployed

3. the software is heavily customized.

The last of these will be covered in great detail later in this report. For this section, we will concentrate upon instances/versions and data centers.

When client sites are implemented (in a geographic roll-out) at a time quite disparate from initial site implementation, it is probable that the enterprise applications vendor has issued upgrades. Thus, site number fifteen may be inclined to implement the new version in order to avoid a consequent upgrade program. However, if the preceding fourteen sites are working on a prior version, such a choice may not be optimal as version differences may be important.

Varying instances or versions can also occur when parts of the client organization resist adopting data hierarchies and/or business processes that have been established at other sites. Instead, new versions or instances are established which, in essence, need to be interfaced to "brother" enterprise applications installations. As these variations proliferate, data coherency declines.

In the case of SAP, for example, it is often advised that clients should not have in excess of three separate instances and yet countless large organizations have more than one hundred and are not capable of consolidating data across the whole.

In fact, one of my clients has more than two hundred instances. Some years ago, they put out a Request for Proposal to all the top SAP systems integration firms asking for help in reducing to less than thirty instances. None of the firms even responded to the RFP as the task was deemed impossible.

By the same token, when data centers proliferate beyond two or three, data maintenance becomes more onerous. A foundational point of enterprise applications is the existence of a single data base for all integrated applications. Thus, in a large organization, master data management is an exceptional challenge that is only further complicated as data centers proliferate.

The figure on the next page illustrates how catering to local or specific concerns will degrade integration across the whole of enterprise applications. When beginning with a highly centralized organization and moving down a spectrum of less centralized organizations to a highly decentralized organization, the results for differing criteria will change.

| Model | | Centralized | | Less Centralized | | Hubbed | | Decentralized | |
|---|---|---|---|---|---|---|---|---|---|
| Criteria | Import | Means | Score | Means | Score | Means | Score | Means | Score |
| Process Integration | 5 | 5 | 25 | 3 | 15 | 2 | 10 | 1 | 5 |
| Process Cost Reduction | 5 | 4 | 20 | 3 | 15 | 1 | 5 | 1 | 5 |
| Lowest Costs | 4 | 5 | 20 | 4 | 16 | 2 | 8 | 2 | 8 |
| Local Business Flexibility | 3 | 2 | 6 | 4 | 12 | 4 | 12 | 5 | 15 |
| Process Flexibility | 3 | 4 | 12 | 3 | 9 | 3 | 9 | 2 | 6 |
| Legacy Retirement | 3 | 1 | 3 | 3 | 9 | 3 | 9 | 4 | 12 |
| Relative Integration | | | 86 | | 76 | | 53 | | 51 |

In the preceding example, local business flexibility and process flexibility are deemed as less important than process integration and cost reduction, for example. Thus, the relative integration is higher when the organization is centralized.

While a fully centralized enterprise applications plant may not be viable, organizations need to establish and maintain a tolerance level that balances individual unit requirements against the imperative for continued integration and consolidation capability.

## Application Portfolio Management

The failure to energetically retire legacy systems will leave an organization with an unnecessary burden of software maintenance for those systems and probable interfacing maintenance to the core enterprise applications.

While clients move to enterprise applications with the intent of replacing legacy systems, the market is rife with clients that fail to adequately retire legacy systems after enterprise applications Go-Live. This occurs primarily because of:

- resistance on the part of stakeholders to conform to newly-adopted processes; such resistance is frequently due to legacy functionality that stakeholders feel they cannot do without and which that cannot be reproduced with enterprise applications

- the failure of an organization to adequately plan and implement legacy retirement

- the failure of an organization to adequately train end users to enterprise applications; as a consequence, end users will continue to use legacy software if it is still available

- "not invented here" – often with the erroneous notion that because a legacy system is customized to a firm's existing processes it is, by definition, a better fit.

A legacy retirement plan should take into account what legacy applications will be retired as of the initial enterprise applications implementation. Many organizations succeed to this point but falter through the course of the initial implementation for the reasons cited above.

Where organizations fail most often is after the initial implementation when momentum cannot be sustained. The plan should also be extended to include subsequent legacy retirement that will occur when a) extended applications are implemented and/or b) when extended functionality can be derived with existing applications (either through configuration or customization).

## Why Firms Need a Center of Excellence

After going live with SAP applications, many client firms struggle through operational issues. Business performance often takes a back seat to day-to-day applications management.

The fact is, too few implementing firms properly plan for post Go-Live operations and fail to refresh their "To-Be" vision. As a result, they are not prepared to seize measurable business benefit from their SAP investment.

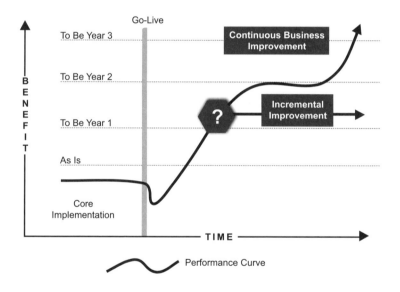

A key element of the new business/IT dynamic is the ability of a client to gain continuous business improvement rather than the incremental gains afforded by the traditional business/IT dynamic.

The full solution to this "as-is rut" is the creation of a Center of Excellence with the following goals in mind:

- An optimization of business processes that drive business benefit continually

- An optimization of end user competency and employee fulfillment of business processes
- Continued coherence and integration of functionality and data through all process chains.

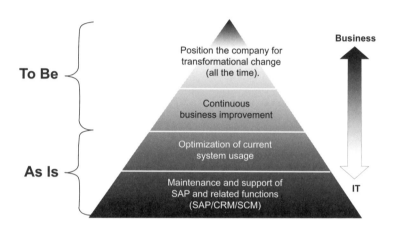

The essential purpose of the Center of Excellence is to drive applications maturity and increase effective applications deployment. As detailed in the preceding chapter, applications are not deemed mature until their evolution is guided by business results (read = business metrics).

The key organizational difference for a client firm moving to a Center of Excellence is the shift of some traditional IT functions into the Center of Excellence, including business process design, integration management, and enterprise applications business functional configuration/programming.

## Center of Excellence Organization

Among the successful centers of excellence I have seen over the past nine years, no two are identical in terms of organization.

What they all have in common are key characteristics:

- Clear lines of communication and authority
- Well defined roles within the Center of Excellence
- Intrinsic business-IT alignment

The organization described below is a base template that will vary according to your firm's size, geographic reach, and applications portfolio. Later in this chapter we provide some variant templates.

Note that the Center of Excellence resides outside the traditional IT organization. In the sample positioning above, it is presumed that the CIO is a "change agent" rather than merely a senior IT official.

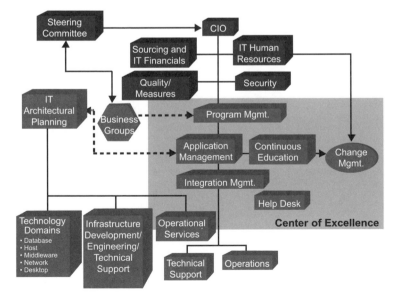

There is nothing especially technical about the Center of Excellence; application management is driven by the lines of business via program management and in turn application management drives continuous education, change management, and integration management.

Further, application management provides input to IT leadership where infrastructure, database, middleware, and the like are affected.

The Center of Excellence is organized as follows:

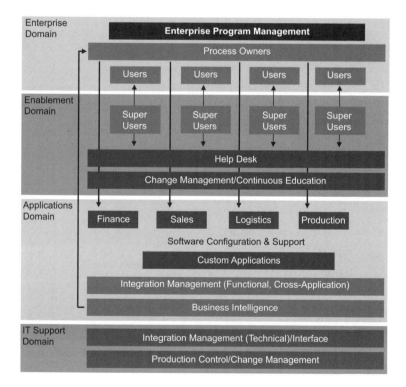

This organization does not have to be housed in the same office or even in the same location. As such, there are untold variations of virtual Centers of Excellence.

Many firms outsource the application and support domains either in whole or in part on the premise that these domains are less strategic than the enterprise and enablement domains. This option is covered in separate chapters of this book.

There are four "domains" that comprise an Enterprise Applications Center of Excellence:

- Enterprise Domain: defines how program and process are managed

- Enablement Domain: defines how end users are prepared and supported

- Application Domain: defines how applications are configured and integrated

- IT Support Domain: defines how integrated applications are maintained and supported

These domains are not discrete or closed-end organizations. Each has some level of interaction with the others, the only exception being that there is no interaction between the enterprise and IT support domains.

## Enterprise Domain

The Center of Excellence is run by the Enterprise Program Management Office (EPMO) or equivalent, which reports to the CIO (or designated change agent) and the IT Steering Committee while receiving its project initiatives from the various business lines. The EPMO drives the vision, strategy, budget, and prioritization for Application Management:

- formal software implementation projects

- directives for specific business process changes or improvements.

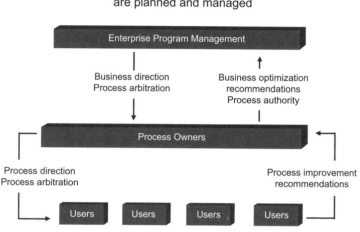

## Enterprise Domain
Enterprise Domain defines how program and process
are planned and managed

Ideally, these initiatives will be driven by Key Performance Indicators as well as traditional business imperatives such as mergers, organizational changes, and event-driven programs. In essence, EPMO is responsible for an evolving To-Be vision.

If your firm does not have an official EPMO, the role defined above can simply be fulfilled by top management.

However, the EPMO also manages enterprise applications portfolio, standards, and measures and sub-manages vendor relationships (high level). These responsibilities would not be carried out by top management.

Process owners address implementation and process issues across Lines of Business and take direction from the CIO (or designated change agent) and the EPMO. Their primary function is to drive continual business process improvements targeting Key Performance Indicator (KPI) improvement. As such, they are primary drivers of the applications management agenda.

Process owners also receive direction in regard to business process improvement from the users and they drive and monitor user competency through Help Desk and Continuous Education.

- respond to enterprise Program Management (top) and user feedback (bottom)

- cross lines of business, which can require process arbitration from the EPMO

- drive the applications agenda

- monitor/drive user competency through Help Desk and Continuous Education

End Users fulfill business processes, change the way they work to support improved business processes, provide feedback to process owners, and tap Power Users for support and first level of problem resolution.

They receive fulfillment support from the help desk and receive relevant continuous training from user support.

- fulfill business processes

- provide feedback to process owners

- tap Help Desk for resolution

- receive continuous training from user support

## Enablement Domain

Power users train new end users and serve as "go-to" people who answer system functionality and business process questions. They also troubleshoot application problems and coach colleagues on the best practices for application deployment. One key purpose of this coaching is to increase user competence in regard to the role of fulfilling business processes and thus contributing to KPI improvement.

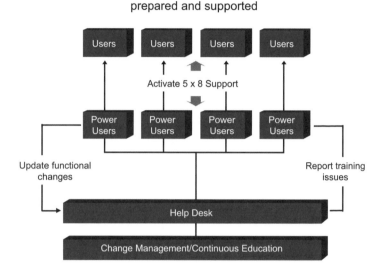

**Enablement Domain**
Enablement Domain defines how end users are
prepared and supported

Power users (AKA super users) also support configuration and programming teams to translate functional business requirements into technical requirements/specifications. Power users may assist in configuration unit and integration tests and usually fulfill user acceptance testing.

Organizational Change Management secures sponsorship of business process change across all stakeholder groups, develops and maintains an integrated change/risk management strategy and training program, and ensures that end-users and business stakeholders are prepared to adopt new ways of work.

Continuous Education develops integrated, role-based training specific to business process configuration. In support of this responsibility, they develop training channels, job aids to support new user roles, deliver initial training, and develops and deliver continuous training Post Go-Live, most pointedly when there are major business process changes and/or applications software upgrades or extensions.

## Applications Domain

Many firms do a fine job of creating and sustaining the Enterprise and Enablement domains. Where they often founder is in regard to the application domain due to either a stubborn IT-centrism in regard to application configuration and maintenance or to a failure to secure direct business collaboration.

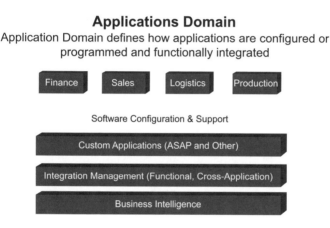

**Applications Domain**

Application Domain defines how applications are configured or programmed and functionally integrated

| Finance | Sales | Logistics | Production |

Software Configuration & Support

Custom Applications (ASAP and Other)

Integration Management (Functional, Cross-Application)

Business Intelligence

The SAP configuration and support team, which resides within application management:

- effects non-customized changes to applications software

- provides functional specification to the custom application engineers both for interfacing requirements to legacy systems or for new custom applications that cannot be engineered through enterprise software configuration

- unit tests software changes

- communicates process and system changes to the continuous education entity in the enablement domain.

This team may participate, with Super Users, in user acceptance testing.

Note that application management is not an IT-centric function. As such, staff assigned to SAP configuration will preferably be derived from the business community. For more in this regard, see the subsection "Mastering the Business-IT Dynamic" later in this chapter.

Integration management is responsible for cross-application integration testing and the handover to the IT support domain for technical integration, change management, and production control. This level of integration management is the nexus between a business-centric Application Management group and the IT support entity.

### IT Support Domain

Business challenges come and go but being shouted at in public tends to linger in the memory. Once, in the course of a presentation to about forty people on this same subject, I was interrupted by an attendee who shouted, "You told us all this last year and we took your advice! We turned configuration over to our business staff and it was a mess! Complete chaos!"

## IT Support Domain

IT Support Domain defines how integrated applications
are supported and promoted to production

Technical Integration Management

Production Control/Technical Change Management

In that one moment I was flattered (hey, the guy took my advice) and alarmed (he did use the word 'chaos').

The point of his anger and disappointment, it turned out, was that business people were also given the authority to promote configuration changes to production. Oops.

Once functional integration is complete, configurations must be turned over to IT. Technical integration is not a business-centric endeavor. This is the only "IT-centric" domain of the four and it is responsible for integration management on a technical level, technical stress testing, promote-to-production, user authorities and security and user/functional monitoring.

The support domain is also on call for error handling/technical help desk (often via vendor) as well both production control and ongoing change management of applications software.

## Transforming the "Build" Team into a Continuous Business Evolution Team

During enterprise application implementation projects, systems integrators join with client IT and business staff to form a project team primarily dedicated to business process design and subsequent configuring of software to fulfill that design. This team is usually complemented by other IT build teams that address reporting, interfacing, data migration, data warehousing, or custom applications.

Most clients erroneously dissolve these teams shortly after Go-Live and revert to a traditional IT maintenance mode that results in an incremental improvement rut and unnecessarily isolates IT from business. To assure continuous business evolution, these teams should remain largely intact, with sufficient resource to not only maintain the initial To Be vision but also to drive evolution through extended applications, renewed business process improvement, and extended user competency.

During an implementation project, most of the Center of Excellence elements are already in working order. Process owners define business design with the applications management team,

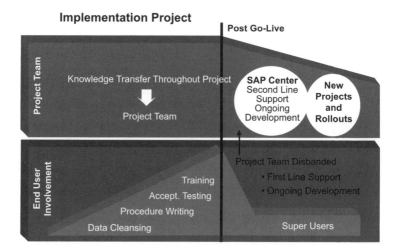

whose software changes are moved to integration management and subsequently production. Just prior to Go-Live, the remaining elements are added, namely help desk and the end user population. Help desk staff and end user groups should be trained not only to the software being implemented, but also to the continuous business evolution methodology inherent in the Center of Excellence.

Presuming you did not follow this path, you will have to transition various of your role-players into a Center of Excellence job description.

| Group/Function | Knowledge Required |
|---|---|
| **Executives** EPMO, steering committee, C-Level: funding, authority, and charter of the Center of Excellence | How they contribute to fulfillment of one or more business processes. Where to go for help and/or more training. Cross-functional software deployment. |
| **End Users** System exploitation, training and re-training, exceptions reporting, user acceptance testing | How they contribute to fulfillment of one or more business processes. Where to go for help and/or more training. Cross-functional software deployment. |
| **Super Users** 5 x 8 support to end users, key contact for process owners | Business process in the context of SAP. Mastery of SAP functionality and tools. Awareness of business intelligence sources. Training skills. |
| **Help Desk** Call Center (front end), functional assistance/referral | System navigation and connectivity troubleshooting, Security tracing, and typical application functional questions to query users when reporting problems. |
| **Process Owners** Monitor business results, define business process improvements | Business/IT integration principles, process flow, SAP module basics, project methodology, business intelligence |
| **Applications Management** Software configuration to fulfill business process improvements, functional design for customization, functional integration testing, user documentation to continuous end user training | LOB business knowledge, business/IT integration principles, SAP configuration, business process flow, workflow, Help Desk procedures, project methodology |
| **IT Support** Production control/change management, middleware administration | Transport control, change management, Hierarchy, instance management |

## New Era, New Skills

Jon Reed has been advising SAP/ERP consultants since 1994 (www.jonerp.com) and is a certified SAP mentor for BPX (business process). He finds that the traditional "module consultant" is more and more required to move past modules and expand into full-blown process consulting. "In the past, it was sufficient for a consultant to be a hyphenate: FI-CO, SD-MM, MM-PP," he relates. "Consultants, both internal and external, are increasingly required to stretch their knowledge not only in terms of a horizontal business process but also in regard to related business measurements at the KPI level."

We agree that traditional 'hyphenates' still have value, especially if they can combine SAP technical skills with strong consulting bones and the requisite business knowledge. We also agree that an individual with a mastery of the Orders to Cash business process, combined with experience in configuring the modules that support that process, is worth gold.

Jon adds, "Speaking of Business Process Experts (or BPXers as they are often referred to in an SAP context), it's important to understand that 'BPX' is not just a vision of where the SAP functional skill set is headed. It's a recognition that IT and business are becoming increasingly intertwined, and the best SAP professionals – the ones your company wants to keep on the softball team – are those chameleons who can walk across the aisle with comfort and talk business or 'tech speak' as needed."

BPXers fall into the crucial realm of business process owners and applications configuration, where business results are directly driven. The old business-asks-IT dynamic is obsolete.

As Jon Reed concludes, "The SAP skills world of the future is a techno-functional convergence, where suits are sometimes geeks and geeks sometimes wear the suits."

## A Note About Basis Administration

Savvy readers will have noted that we do not include Basis functions within the Center of Excellence. This not because we consider the functions to be trivial but because they do not fit into the charter of a Center of Excellence (business process excellence leading to measurable business benefit).

In the following pages are more precise job descriptions, all of which will necessarily vary depending upon your staff size, organization, and the charter of your Center of Excellence.

## Center of Excellence: Thumbnail Job Descriptions

### Executive Level/Steering Committee:

Fund, authorize, charter, and champion the Center of Excellence as the foundation for continually gaining value from the SAP/enterprise applications investments.

Provide direction to the EPMO in regard to company strategy and direction as a foundation for program management office budgets and priorities.

Where necessary, arbitrate cross-business issues arising from business process owners.

### Enterprise Program Management Office:

In the context of strategic direction from the executive level/steering committee, identify strategic cross-functional issues which SAP can enable e.g. opportunities to gain efficiencies.

Provide direction to the SAP Business Process Leaders regarding business priorities and timelines.

Authorize budgets and monitor costs of application management, change management, and continuous training functions.

Arbitrate business process ownership issues.

### Business Process Owners:

Assess and monitor process performance and metrics with a focus upon continuous process improvement.

Assess end user input regarding process improvement

Identify additional action items as needed to achieve continuous process improvement.

Maintain detailed knowledge of processes within assigned departments, and understand how processes transcend department boundaries and impact other functions within the organization.

Identify process/procedural changes to measurably improve overall process performance at KPI level.

Work with business stakeholders to clarify and ensure linkage between system enhancements and business process benefits.

Work with other Process Owners and Business Leaders to assess cross-functional process metrics and performance.

In conjunction with the change management/continuous training group, regularly assess end user competency and provide directives for raising the level.

Conduct feasibility studies for SAP system enhancements, evaluate system design, and determine cost/benefit and economic justification.

Review/evaluate the capabilities of existing systems for conformance to standards and maintain a clear understanding of the system development and maintenance life cycle.

Serve as an SAP expert; advise colleagues on improved ways to use the system; act as a "first line of support" for SAP related problems.

## Super Users

A super user is an end user who has in-depth knowledge and understanding of SAP system and respective business processes utilizing SAP. This individual serves as "go to" person within the function to answer specific department-related system functionality and business process questions.

Troubleshoots SAP-related problems and coaches colleagues on using the system.

Supports configuration specialists and helps to translate functional business requirements into technical requirements/specifications.

Communicates configuration/functionality changes to the business.

Participates in end user acceptance testing.

Trains new end-users.

Keeps his/her knowledge of the system in their specific area up-to-date.

Contributes to the on-going process development.

Reports system problems/requests for enhancements to applications management.

## Application Management Leadership

(Large organizations may well have discrete leadership roles. Smaller organizations will have staff with combined application leadership and functional responsibilities)

Application leadership is the first-line contact for business process owners on one side and configuration support on the other. An application leader acts as project manager in terms of resource scheduling and assignments, budget/actual tracking, adherence to configuration/programming standards, and supervision of end user acceptance testing and functional integration testing.

## Application Management Staff

Coordination of new SAP releases.

Development and continued maintenance of SAP Business Process Procedures, Functional Specifications, Unit Test Scripts, Integration Test Scripts and other associated documents.

Create SAP Change Requests and Tasks using the Transport Organizer.

Enter configuration changes into SAP Development System.

Perform unit test and integration test of new and modified configurations.

Write functional specifications for new and changed interfaces.

Assist in unit and integration test of new and changed interfaces with bolt-on software.

Assist training department in development and maintenance of training materials.

Assist in performance and stress testing in conjunction with the Basis Administration team.

Troubleshoot SAP configuration problems. Coordinate changes to SAP based on OSS findings with the Basis Team.

Determination of training impact from new SAP releases (evaluate training delta requirements).

Coordination of updated SAP Business Process Procedures and related training documents to end-users.

Coordinate continuing transports and refreshes for training clients (including Sandbox).

Monitor configuration changes into SAP Development System and determine impact on training materials and delta delivery (if required).

Perform continual updates (as needed) to training tools: Knowledge Warehouse and On Demand (if applicable).

## Variant Structures for Centers of Excellence

The organizational structure of a Center of Excellence will vary depending upon a client's application portfolio and site management.

Below is a high-level example for a firm with one or more sites that have some functional or business process variations.

In this example, there is still a centralized help desk and the continuous education team provides support remotely.

In the remote locations, process oversight is relative to local process variations (e.g. orders to cash) and functional oversight is relative to local functional variations (e.g. methods for posting cash receipts).

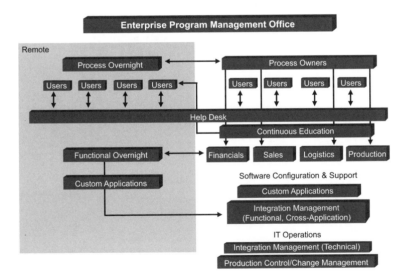

This variant addresses a smaller organization that does not require a formal EPMO. Line of Business leaders provide input and direction to a business process management entity charged with coordinating and integrating LOB business requirements and providing specifications, priorities, and requirements to a vendor governance group.

In this scenario, vendor governance manages two suppliers: an applications support group charged with providing user support and ongoing applications support and a hosting/support group charged with applications operations and Basis support.

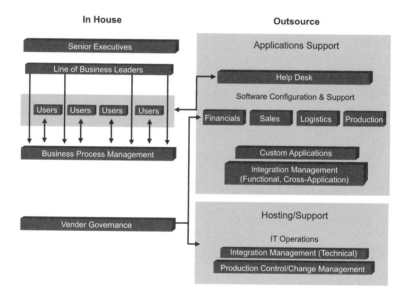

## Mastering the Business/IT Dynamic

Successful SAP life-cycle management is dependent upon a healthy business/IT dynamic in which goals are aligned and with which IT supports are highly responsive to business change.

In this light, a new dynamic must replace the traditional organization between IT and business in which business personnel request IT services, define needs to IT representatives, then await tested and implemented new or revised software.

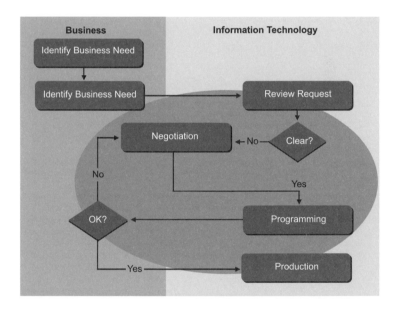

In the traditional dynamic, business makes requests to IT and is required to negotiate design and deadline. Negotiations and consequent programming/testing often have to be repeated and this iterative loop is a) extremely costly, b) at the heart of business-IT antagonism, and c) sloooow. Such a dynamic is nearly inevitable for legacy applications because they are program-based. If you have SAP and are still stuck in this dynamic, you have wasted a prime opportunity to evolve.

When both sides are collaborative, such a dynamic can function. However, let's be honest. This dynamic has been in place since the early 1960's. It consists of bargaining, negotiation, business people suspicious of IT terminology and IT people suspicious of business needs. The result is often rancor. In short, this dynamic is at the heart of the failure to align business and IT.

"I wanted a horse and got a cow."

"The business people can't say clearly what they want."

"IT is too slow."

"The business people can't agree on their direction."

A more business-centric dynamic can be attained for enterprise applications because they are configuration-based and much of the configuration can be accomplished by business staff.

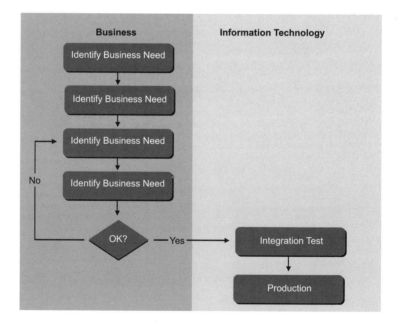

## A Word about Solution Manager

SAP Solution Manager is the SAP-approved NetWeaver tool for managing and sustaining your SAP applications. The focus of SAP Solution Manager is your SAP software platform, not your organization. In that light, a fully functional Solution Manager is as beneficial to SAP as it is to you in that their maintenance is vastly simplified.

Mark Dendinger recommends deployment of this asset. "Solution Manager can streamline a client's SAP performance management, thus liberating resources to concentrate on more strategic tasks."

The key benefits of Solution Manager should be:

1. Enhanced visibility to SAP support. (While Solution Manager benefits clients, it also vastly reduces the burden of SAP support)

2. Enhanced visibility and control of SAP deployment (service level reporting, diagnostics, change control...)

If Solution Manager is deployed in the course of an implementation, seizing these benefits is a fairly straightforward endeavor. However, many clients and consultants have reported difficulties in retrofitting Solution Manager to an existing SAP installation. The steps required for this process are highly technical and thus do not fall under the charter of this book. Again, the Center of Excellence described in this chapter is focused upon gaining vibrant business and IT alignment directed towards gaining measurable business benefit. While an efficient SAP software platform will clearly enhance your chances of success, the SAP Solution Manager is not crucial to this definition of a Center of Excellence.

## What Goes Wrong: How Centers of Excellence Become Centers of Mediocrity

### Leadership and Entropy:

At about the time I got my start in the SAP world, I was heavily influenced by a wonderful short book, *Management of the Absurd, Paradoxes in Leadership* by Richard Farson. In lively, witty, and elegant prose, Mr. Farson exposes a number of illusions about management and leadership and provides insight into why organizations fall into entropy. In my experience with SAP installed base organizations, I have observed firsthand a number of these illusions and their deleterious effects.

Newly-minted centers of excellence tend to sputter and disintegrate within mere months due to an over-reliance upon leadership, vision, and nifty organization charts. "Joe was our leader. He was a great motivator and kept things together. Joe's not here any more and we are back to the drawing board."

Resignations, reorganizations, mergers, and office politics can all lead to changes in your Center of Excellence but business results just keep happening. No entropy there. What holds a Center of Excellence together, what is in fact an excellent *center,* is an organizational (all hands) understanding of how business results direct your activities.

"Our customer satisfaction level was low (measure) due to slow delivery (measure). Our order fulfillment process was taking nine days (measure) so we streamlined the process down to six (measure) and client satisfaction rose ten points (measure).""Client complaints about our design process had nearly doubled (measure). We put our key clients on a portal for direct communication with our engineers. Pre-orders tripled (measure)."

This is (worrisome) cause and (positive) effect having little to do with leadership and everything to do with facing a key performance indicator (customer satisfaction) and directly addressing it. Business intelligence is the leader here, not Joe. And business intelligence can always be there whereas Joe may not be.

## Business Process Orphanship

The notion of business process was popularized in the mid-1990's by the bestseller *Reengineering the Corporation* by James Champy and Michael Hammer. However, it is difficult for many companies to shift an organizational mindset away from discrete vertical departments (marketing-sales-production-billing) into fully operational and horizontal business process units. Therefore, the role of business process ownership is only partially baked into the business conscience and fulfilling that role can be perilous.

Since most business processes cross departmental boundaries, their "owners" are often at odds with department heads with turf issues. Without a clear charter and authority from on high, a business process owner is constantly buffeted by resistance to process change. The result is an inability to improve business processes beyond the tinkering stage which does not result in any appreciable business benefit. In such a situation, business process ownership is business process orphanship.

Back when I was first researching best practices for post-implementation SAP, I had the good fortune to work with Jack Childs of SAP America whose task in life was supporting the major North American SAP accounts and whose insight into client efforts was invaluable. In 2003, Mr. Childs administered an informal poll regarding the role of a business process owner and found that the shelf-life was only two years. Reasons for this short shelf life were unsurprising: high stress, low authority, inability to succeed.

If you do not invest good business process owners with proper executive support, you should not bother building a Center of Excellence. Of all the roles included, it is the most vital.

## Super Users Cast Adrift

Many years ago, I was on a long call with a Gateway technician helping me to save my hard drive. While various operations were running, she regaled me with stories, either lived or recounted by others, of strange help desk calls. The client whose foot-pedal didn't work. It was the mouse. The client whose cup holder was broken. The CD tray. The client who only got a black screen. The video wasn't plugged in. And finally, everyone's favorite: the client who for the life of him could not find the Any key.

The hour I spent with the Gateway technician cost my company nothing nor were the aforementioned callers charged for their queries because none of us were using in-house help desk. For those of you with an in-house SAP help desk, we have to ask the question: how much of your time is spent explaining that a mouse is not a foot pedal and a CD tray is not a cup holder?

On many occasions, I have had the fascinating task of assessing a client's SAP help desk statistics. Call volume, average call time, average resolution time, and the like are invariably categorized but I have yet to see the category "mindless waste of time" so I have no statistical handle on the frequency of such calls in an SAP environment.

However, there has been one simple trend to every help desk analysis I have ever been a part of and that is the very high percentage of calls that relate to "end user training." That is to say, calls that would not be necessary if end users were properly trained and supported.

According to a 2008 study by Insite Objects, 72% of firms with SAP have some form of super user organization. Our observation is that the life span and utility of super users varies from place to place. The importance of super users cannot be understated. When properly motivated and deployed, they raise end user competency and consequent business benefit of SAP deployment.

The proper ratio of super users to end users is 1 to 10 or 20. Super users should be available for one-on-one coaching, group update training, and some level of analysis regarding what might be done to improve over-all end user competency.

The super user function is not full-time and managers often feel that employee time given over to this function is lost. The pressures on super users include a) demanding front-line jobs that leave inadequate time to fulfill the super user role, b) lack of management support, c) inadequate documentation or tools for ongoing SAP training, and d) faulty or over-specialized business processes that render SAP functions too clunky and hard to talk up. When these pressures come to bear, super users drop their gloves and stick close to their front-line jobs.

Without the support of support users, individual end users:

- Will not keep up their SAP skills

- Will not extend their SAP skills

- Will feel burdened whenever there are changes to processes or functions.

A few of my former colleagues have long labored selling SAP end user training courses. The value of their courseware is huge but that value is chronically rejected. Years ago, in a study of 120 firms in the installed base, two of my questions were:

1. Who in your firm is responsible for SAP end user competency?

2. Who in your firm controls the budget for SAP end user training?

When responses were expressed in bar charts, the bars for "Don't Know" and "No One" towered over the others (IT director, HR director, VP of ERP, CIO, et al).

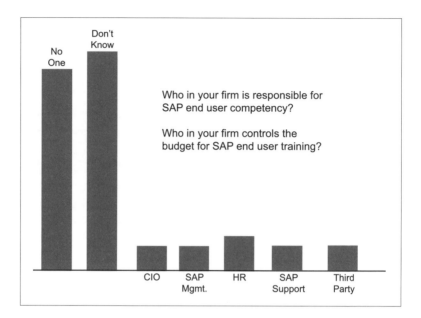

Something like shown above:

A help desk is a great start toward resolving this issue. At base, the distinction between help desk and super users is that help desk is AAA and super users are the GPS. Lost or misdirected users cost money and fail to effectively fulfill business processes. This is precisely how your SAP return-on-investment goes right out the side door while you are gazing at the ceiling.

## Burial by SAP

Through the years, SAP has persistently offered add-on software, tools, or middleware intended to help clients raise their maturity of SAP deployment. The aforementioned Solution Manager is one of these offerings. While there are arguments in favor of their value, I find that many clients tend to get buried in the technology issues promoted by SAP at the expense of business focus. The Center of Excellence described in this chapter is a "beyond systems" vision, albeit in a context enabled by SAP applications software.

As previously mentioned, many firms have Centers of Excellence that have a more SAP-centric charter. In past years, SAP has presented various initiatives relative to SAP Competency Center, SAP Customer Care Center, and the like, and in every case the subject was *more efficient deployment of SAP software.* Fair enough but this is a subset of the larger and more cogent subject: business results.

CHAPTER 4

# We Do It Themselves:
# Outsourcing SAP Applications Support

# We Do It Themselves: Outsourcing SAP Applications Support and Basis Support

## Applications Are What We Do

Early in the millennium, I was asked by a number of clients what service providers could help them to plan and build a Center of Excellence. To get a handle on these requests, I contacted SAP leaders at all of the usual suspects (Accenture, Deloitte, IBM, BearingPoint, and CapGemini) as well as a number of second tier firms. All initially assured me that they provided such a service but all hedged dramatically when pressed for a methodology, references, and costing. Instead I was invariably ushered into a meeting with the head of a nascent applications outsourcing practice where I was assured that applications outsourcing was the wave of the future.

Thwarted in my attempt to find firms that could build SAP centers of excellence, I turned my attention back to clients to see how interested they'd be in outsourcing their applications.

During a presentation on post-implementation SAP strategies to a group of META Group clients in Chicago, I was asked again if servicer providers had a methodology and service offering for helping build them. No, I replied, but they would offer to take over the applications in an outsourcing environment. To gauge audience interest I asked for a show of hands of those who would consider outsourcing the management of their SAP applications. No hands were raised but many voices were heard. Whatever SAP creditation I had earned to that point in the presentation was largely lost as both my wisdom and sanity were questioned. I especially remember a VP of IT laughing loudly and remarking, "Applications are what we do."

About a year later, we did some primary research that indicated fully 41% of respondents would not even consider outsourcing their applications. This part of our research was a standard "adoption scale" in which respondents told us in what time-frame they might consider adopting a given technology or service. We had never seen such a high percentage of "will not consider."

While resistance is still extant, service providers continue to offer application outsourcing, which is called by various names: application maintenance outsourcing (AMO), application management outsourcing (also AMO), or application management services (AMS). Yes, another confusing set of three letter acronyms and the letter that bothers potential clients the most is that big M, as in management. It would help immeasurably if the vendors simply offered support.

In more recent years, client acceptance of the service has risen as the notion of "applications are what we do" has morphed into "why are we maintaining these applications ourselves?"

Service provider quality remains mixed, primarily because too many of the service providers have poor or unproven delivery models. More on this to follow.

If you have not considered outsourcing your applications, this chapter should challenge you to do so. If you are already considering outsourcing your applications, this chapter should provide you a roadmap.

For the sake of clarity, I will be addressing two levels of application outsourcing:

> **Application Maintenance:** basic applications hosting/operations, break/fix, debug, backup, etc. (Keeping the lights on)

> **Application Management:** maintenance functions (above) plus a level of application improvement, upgrade, and/or business process transformation. (Expanding the span of light).

For the latter, there are various levels of management:

- Functional application enhancement as needed to assure basic *continuity*

- Frequent application enhancements to provide some *optimization*

- Defined levels/stages of business process *transformation*

The difference between optimization and transformation is enormous. In optimization mode, you are improving the as-is state of your applications. In transformation, you are moving to another to-be state. Optimization is like tuning your car; transformation is like getting a whole new car.

When people say "applications are what we do," they are thinking more about optimization and transformation than about continuity. In this regard, a key misconception regarding the outsourcing of applications support is that clients are "giving it up" when in point of fact they may be giving up redundant, low-level, non-strategic labor while still keeping both hands on the applications steering wheel. There is still a capital W to the We do it themselves proposition.

## Why on Earth Would We Outsource our Applications?

The key value statements offered by a plethora of application outsourcers usually center upon a) economy and b) superior SAP skills.

Whatever the veracity of these statements, it is probable that you are looking for something else. Perhaps the cost of maintaining your SAP applications is acceptable but not predictable due to occasional spikes in demand. Perhaps your internal SAP staff is competent but you are chronically short of some key skills.

Below are some of the key advantages and disadvantages to SAP application outsourcing.

| Outsourced Application Management | | Client Staff (In-House) | |
| --- | --- | --- | --- |
| Advantage | Disadvantage | Advantage | Disadvantage |
| Steeped in method and consulting skills. | No direct stake in operational success (unless contractually). | Direct stake in operational success. | Less knowledge of method and consulting skills. |
| Costs may be shared across multiple clients on an as-needed or as-used basis. | May lack single client focus. | Single client focus is assured. | Costs are not flexed according to usage. |
| Deeper product experience. | | | Shallow product experience. |
| Better exposure to industry best practices. | Not deeply oriented to client business context and organization. | Fully oriented to client business context and organization. | |
| | May not have the capacity/skills to manage a mix of enterprise and legacy applications. | Greater experience with legacy applications. | Less exposure to industry best practices. |
| Deeper knowledge of business process design. | | | Shallow knowledge of business process design. |

This on the one hand but on the other hand stuff can lead to circular debates so you might want to weight the relative importance of each of the variables. Taking them one at a time.

If your in-house staff is chronically weak at methodology and people skills, outside resource may be a boon. As for a direct stake in operational success, your in-house people have face time that an outside provider will not. Having said that, with good governance, you can be sure that your provider will have a stake in your success.

One major advantage to outsourcing of applications, especially in an on-demand environment, is the economy of resource coupled with predictability of service. Many firms assign in-house SAP staff to support roles and project roles on a 50-50 percent basis only to find this type of scenario occurs:

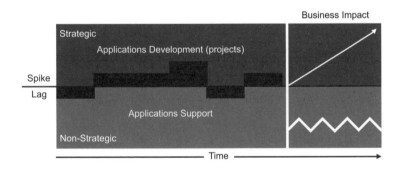

Applications support is a little bit like ER and SAP installations have their "full moons" so the predictability of support demand is compromised as well as staff availability for projects.

On the subject of product experience (relative to SAP), service providers do not always have more depth. A client of mine once complained that a potential provider claimed five plus years of SAP experience on average. "We've had SAP for ten years," she told me, "and most of my staff is still with me."

If your SAP applications are heavily customized and/or heavily interfaced with other applications, this uniqueness will hamper your ability to outsource more than one or two support levels (see following).

If you are contracting for applications management, business process skills come into play. While in-house staff knows your business process better than outsiders, the outsiders will normally have greater knowledge of the best business processes due to greater client exposure. Outsiders may also have better insight as to how you link business performance metrics to business processes.

From direct experience and through primary research, these are the three reasons that are most often cited for outsourcing SAP applications support:

1. Bridge a skills/expertise gap

2. Provide more predictable cost and business response

3. Free up staff from banal maintenance to concentrate upon more strategic issues

Reasons 1 and 2 are fairly obvious. Reason 3 goes deeper than it looks.

After the first great wave of SAP implementations arrived on the post-Y2K shore, there was a glut of underemployed SAP consultants across the United States and many found refuge by returning to industry in a maintenance role. For most of these people, boredom quickly set in. Without the adrenalin of project-based work – the challenges, the deadlines, the pressing need to constantly upgrade their skills – they found themselves turning into clock watchers and could not wait for the market to pick up so they could head back out into the field.

There are similar effects for in-house staff if the day-to-day work is a) maintaining interfaces, b) de-bugging, and c) responding to user queries. What we see is a split of duties between exciting new stuff (a small percentage) and boring daily maintenance (a large percentage). While the notion of "applications is what we do" has its merits, I think what we mean is closer to "improving and expanding applications are what we want to do." Without "at hand" outside help As-Is has a persistent way of trumping To-Be.

## Smart-Sourcing

Resource allocation for SAP support is two parts science and one part guesswork. For that reason, one good strategy is to reserve a percentage of your budget for outside help on the premise that you cannot know with full precision exactly what resource you will need in the future.

For example, if you have a budget of $1M for support resource, you might have six full-time staff costing $700K and a support contract for $300K that provides you 3,000 hours (75 weeks) that you can tap as you need. Spike requirements for reporting? Basis questions that your staff can't address? Surprise projects?

Open-ended sourcing across the spectrum from FI-CO to SD, MM, PP, QM, Basis, or even project management will provide you with flexibility and continuity while assuring that you are not over-staffed in a given discipline.

## Application Outsourcing Adoption

In this section, we will explore ways to assess your organizational readiness to outsource your applications to some level (either maintenance or management). While such an assessment may well point to your lack of readiness, it should also provide a diagnostic as to how you can be ready.

On the following page is an adoption model from your internal organizational alignment to execution of the service:

For each of the five stages of adoption, there are four key focus categories:

*State of Applications:* how reasonable is it to presume that outsiders can maintain your applications? If they are extremely unique (i.e. highly customized, heavily interfaced) or in disarray, handover will be compromised.

*Environment/Risk/Change Management:* careful targeting of applications to be outsourced and how that outsourcing should occur are at the heart of outsourcing success. Particular attention should be given to planning forward governance of the to-be-chosen vendor.

*End Users and Supports:* the key constituents of outsourced application maintenance are the users. Therefore, preparing them and including them in outsource planning is highly recommended.

*Skills:* this category of activity is a combination of a) assessing what skills must be retained in-house for strategic activities and what skills are needed from an outsourcing vendor and b) preparation of individuals to effectively perform vendor governance.

The five levels of adoption do not have to be completed sequentially but an agreed-upon point of closure for each level should be met.

## SAP Application Outsourcing Adoption Model

| Level | State of Applications | Environment/ Change Management | End Users and Support | Skills |
|---|---|---|---|---|
| 1 Aligned | Applications to be outsourced are fully implemented and required interfacing is complete. | Determination of specific applications under consideration and applications not to be outsourced. | End users and super users are identified. | Identification of specific skills sets associated with applications is complete. |
| 2 Assessed | Have acceptable levels of a) customization and b) quality, nature, and volume of interfacing. | Goals and objectives of application outsourcing are established and measured. | Help desk traffic and end user competency have been assessed. | Determination of cost of skills associated with specific application(s) (e.g. prof. development, training, retention, and recruiting). |
| 3 Planned | Final determination of the level of outsourcing to be contracted has been agreed. | Vendor governance relative to business process change (and consequent change management) is in place. | Super user input regarding planned services has been provided. | Identification and selection of potential governance team has been made. |
| 4 Selected | Blueprint of applications management roles and processes is complete. | Outsourcing staff are vetted, contract and due diligence are complete, and transition plan is in place. | Super users agree with vendor selection and transition plan. | Governance team and transitioning staff have met with chosen provider. |
| 5 Executed | Application migration to service provider commences, provider assumes responsibility for application deployment, availability and management. | Contract signed, transition plan begins, risk mitigation processes exercised, employee transition occurs. | Application support requests are successfully routed, logged, and addressed. | Transition, retention, outplacement, and retooling are complete. |

### Aligned

Clients attain this level only if the key constituents (business stakeholders, SAP support team, and the user community) are on the same page. Firms need to address why they should consider outsourcing, candidate functions or areas to be outsourced, and the desired results to be achieved through outsourcing. High level business case formulation, risk assessment and goal formulation are at the core of this level.

### Assessed

Completion of this level is categorized through base case assessment of capabilities/functions in consideration for outsourcing. These assessments examine current base costs and projected future costs of providing these services internally. Factors to consider include: uniqueness of the function to the business (current and projected); skills retention and development (current and projected); comparison (benchmark) to current market offerings.

### Defined

The defined phase begins with the selection of specific functions to outsource and continues through business case development, risk assessment and mitigation planning, service provider identification, and bid process development. Expectations are level-set regarding original intentions and objectives for outsourcing. Internal sourcing team and governance teams are established.

### Selected

This level is completed when the vendor selection is completed. The sourcing team has reviewed competitive bids, compared to base case and scenario planning conducted in assessment and planning phases, vendors have completed due diligence surrounding the function to be outsourced, the client has received a best and final offer. Vendors are evaluated on: Competitiveness (to each other and market prices established during assessment phase), responsiveness, manageability, and adaptability.

## Executed

This phase is characterized by the establishment and implementation of governance policies, procedures, processes and controls as part of contractual execution (formal conclusion of the deal). To satisfactorily complete this level, a client should establish an initial service level agreement (and language affording modification), definition of services to be provided (including line item pricing), benchmarking clauses and timelines, change, problem, incident, and escalation management procedures.

---

What you do not want to do is what a depressingly high percentage of clients do: make it up as you go. Even worse is simply deciding to outsource and immediately searching for a provider. Following a reasonable adoption model may well lead you to conclude that it is not feasible or desirable to outsource your applications support. Following a random adoption model will certainly lead to future problems managing your provider or lead you to drop the idea altogether, whatever its merits.

## Crossing the Bridge from Maintenance to Management

Many clients are far more comfortable outsourcing simply the maintenance of applications rather than the management.

In a maintenance environment, the client still holds the baton and controls the sheet music while a service provider takes care of the orchestra members.

In a management environment, the client still holds the baton but a service provider writes the requested tunes and provides the sheet music to the orchestra. In essence, the client maintains control over what is to be done to applications but cedes control in terms of how.

**Level One**

| Applications Help Desk | Applications "How To" |

**Level Two**

| Applications Support | Applications Continuity and Quality |

**Level Three**

| Application Management | Advanced Applications |

Various providers offer varying levels of support and they tend to break down as follows (contents are partial and vary from vendor to vendor):

### Level 1: Applications Help Desk

1. Respond to end user/super user queries regarding features/functions (applications "how to")

2. Maintain end user documentation

3. Report/diagnostics to level two and three applications support staff

## Level 2: Applications Support

1. De-bug/patch defective applications via configuration or customization

2. Test and apply SAP updates/patches relative to applications

3. Extended remote end user training

4. Upgrade support (testing, loading, and production of SAP upgrade version)

## Level 3: Applications Management

1. Custom reporting via ABAP or relevant SAP tool (SAPscript, BI, et al)

2. SAP application systems extensions via configuration and/or customization

   • extension or improvement of existing application

   • new application

   • SAP approved bolt-on

3. Interfacing between SAP and legacy/other applications

4. End user training relative to application extension or improvement

5. Knowledge transfer to client SAP support team relative to extension or improvement

6. Updated user and technical documentation relative to extension or improvement

7. Extended upgrade support (strategy, blueprinting, configuration, testing, production)

8. Audit/compliance support (often included in level 2)

In many cases, application management can simply be handled through a combination of help desk and periodic staff augmentation services.

Some vendors actually suggest that you even give up the baton and just let them run the applications in *toto*. Such an arrangement leaves the client fully dependent upon the vendor which strikes me as the sinker part that follows hook and line.

Further, returning to the theme of "applications are what we do," take a look at the list of applications management tasks and consider which, if any, are in the wheelhouse of strategic activities.

Moving directly from full in-house applications support to full-blown applications management may not be a wise move. A popular alternative is the Big Toe approach by which clients start out with application maintenance (help desk for users, issues management, and some report writing) and gradually extend the outsourcing footprint. Following the SAP Application Outsourcing Adoption Model, you can best decide to what level you should begin outsourcing during the Alignment and Assessment steps.

## Local and Remote Delivery Models

I am using the term "local" loosely here. Only in rare instances does your outsourcing vendor actually place all of it delivery staff in your location. In this context, think of local as within your cultural and geographic domain despite the fact that the services provided come from a remote location, even when that location is across the street.

Level 1 Help desk is straightforward. An authorized end user calls a help number or enters an issue into a help desk website. The issue is acknowledged, classified, prioritized, and resolved (usually in less than an hour). Many of these issues are resolved in the course of an initial phone call.

More complex issues will be routed directly to level 2 support for resolution. Level 2 issues usually take from one to eight business hours for resolution.

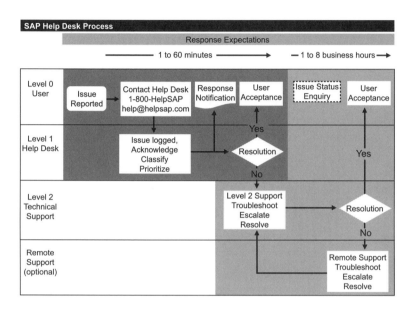

Any term that creates more confusion than clarity should be scrapped and this applies to the term, "offshore." As it happens, this expression is only used in North America. Elsewhere, the realm of services that can be supplied from any remote location is referred to as global sourcing. Even this term can be misleading. If you are located in Boston and your SAP applications support provider is in South Dakota, it is certainly not offshore and very probably not global.

I therefore settle on the term "remote" for services that are provided from outside your cultural and/or geographic boundaries.

In T*he New SAP Blue Book, A Concise Business Guide to the World of SAP,* I describe a local/remote combination of delivery resource for new implementations that can be very beneficial. While a mix of local and remote resource for SAP support can also be beneficial, a different set of considerations apply. The most important of these revolves around a continuous need for effective communication. In an implementation setting, end users are not contacting remote sites for assistance and it is the initial end user-help desk relationship that is at the heart of successful SAP outsourced support.

Note that in the preceding diagram, a level 2 issue can be consigned to a remote support site for resolution. Suppliers that provide both local and remote support are able to a) directly address a client in a comfortable cultural and geographic setting (same language, time-zone, etc.) and b) where needed, tap into a deeper and more diverse remote talent pool that will also cost less than the local resource. (Rates vary from country to country and firm to firm but a thumbnail comparison is that a qualified U.S.-based applications support consultant will cost from $120 to $160 per hour, or at least twice the rate of a qualified "remote" applications support consultant).

When people talk or write about "cheap off-shore resource," they usually fail to comprehend that such the deployment of this resource varies considerably. It is one thing to e-mail specifications from Boston to Shanghai for java programming and quite another to perform business process design between a Boston client and a Shanghai consultant.

When using a local/remote supplier for SAP applications support, a client should insist upon the deployment of a proven web-based communications platform. E-mails and phone calls should be kept to a minimum. "Visibility" is the keyword as a client should be able to see, at any time:

1. Pending issues (by type, priority, and point of origin)

2. Scheduling (resource, estimated resolution time)

3. Closed/resolved issues log

4. Rolling costs

5. Document repository (general documents and indexed to issues)

This is the information a client needs in any case, whether the help desk resource is on Mars or one floor up.

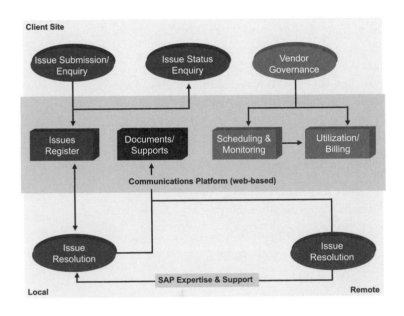

In addition to a robust communications platform, an SAP applications support supplier should also provide rich statistics that will drive a diagnostic emanating from help desk activity. As elaborated further on, I have long observed a very high percentage of help desk tickets relate to training issues.

## Governance for Outsourced SAP Applications Support

Failure to manage your vendor will lead quickly and directly to failure. This is not because the service providers will take advantage of you (though they might) but more because, without your governance, the service providers will not be positioned to succeed for you. Two ugly phrases that persist in this marketplace: *Vendor:* Your Mess for Less. *Client:* We Can Throw All This Over the Wall.

Unless yours is a fairly small organization, you will necessarily have more than one person involved in vendor governance. Below are the four key subject areas of vendor governance:

**Relationship Governance:** daily

- Executive steering: keeping the vendor aware of current priorities or business issues

- Problem resolution: following end user satisfaction

- Service request process: assuring that communications between users and vendor support are functional

- Escalation process: supervision or monitoring of exceptional issues

**Performance Processes:** weekly

- Service-level tracking and reporting: a credible vendor will provide credible reporting on at least a weekly basis

- Service-level review: vendor reports should be validated with the user community

- Benchmarking: performance thresholds can be modified to spur improvement (see fee strategies)

**Contract Processes:** quarterly or bi-annual

- Negotiation management

- Contract management

- Contractor management
- Scope change process

**Technical Processes:** as-needed

- Production acceptance and change management: this applies to configuration changes and thus to an application management scenario
- Governance compliance
- Architectural compliance

All of the above speaks to governance but it really comes down to governing; by that I mean that having the structure and the necessary paperwork will give you a framework but actually *performing* the governance is what matters most.

If your firm is also outsourcing hosting and/or Basis administration, your governance on the technical end may be multi-vendor which will require a second level of governance focusing on the vendor-to-vendor relationship. This does not have to be complex as the relationship between application management and technical teams is identical to that described in chapter "Building and Sustaining a Center of Excellence."

## Fee Strategies

While there are a variety of fee models for application support, the majority in play are fixed-fee and include:

A standard fixed-fee for a packet of pre-determined hours

A standard hourly fee for time in excess of the base amount

The obvious weakness of such an arrangement is that clients may pay for unused time but will always pay when that time is exceeded.

The way around this is to arrange a fixed fee that takes into account three-to-six month averages rather than simply month-to-month. Thus, if a vendor spends less than the allotted time in some months and more in others, costs will balance out to client benefit.

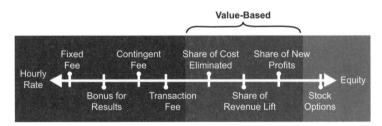

In essence, what you get with a **fixed fee** is some predictability of cost but that is all you get. Service providers working on a fixed fee have little financial motivation to do anything more than deliver the proscribed services. This is a subject where I often cut bait with service providers, especially when they claim a desire to be a "partner" with their clients.

To promote partnership status, clients should consider fee models to the right of fixed fee on the chart above. Paying a **bonus for good results** (e.g. high percent of call resolutions in short time-frames) will provide vendor motivation but such an arrangement should be counterbalanced by getting a credit back for bad results (e.g. low percent of call resolutions and/or long time-frames).

Some clients have exhibited a preference for paying a **transaction fee,** a more on-demand approach by which each help desk ticket is billed individually by time spent. The unpredictable nature of client demand in this regard leads providers to charge higher hourly rates than for a fixed-fee arrangement.

**Gain-sharing methods** lead to the highest level of client-vendor partnership since providers are motivated to help clients reduce costs and/or raise revenues. The down side of such arrangements is that measurement is required and this is an area in which most clients are weak.

Further, gain-sharing fee models lend themselves primarily to application management and strategic efforts as opposed to application maintenance/keeping the lights on.

The simplest method to govern is fixed-fee with some sort of risk/ reward kicker based upon support results in which the initial bar is set at whatever support levels were provided in-house (before transition to the provider). Clients seeking to continually raise this bar should remember that there are, quite naturally, diminishing opportunities to improve. For example, if an initial benchmark for closing out help desk issues is 95% and a service provider improves that figure to 98%, the benchmark should not be going up.

If you are seeking cost reductions, the local/remote model can be very attractive provided a) there is sufficient local resource for language and cultural comfort and b) a solid web-based communications platform.

One final note about fee strategies: you should be getting some form of concession based upon the length of contract. While this may seem obvious, it is not always the case in the real world. An important negotiating point for new adopters is that if you start out with a one-year contract, you should include wording to the effect that an extension, prior to completion of the first year, will result in, at minimum, no raise in fees for the extension period. The point of this is that after the first year, a client may well be a captive audience and thus vulnerable to price hikes for years two, three, and beyond.

## We Do It Themselves

The notion of having everything under the IT sun accomplished in-house arose in the 1970's with the advent of what were then called mini-computers, prominently supplied by firms such as Digital Equipment and Data General. (I started my career in 1974 on Digital Equipment's PDP-11). Prior to the availability of mini-computers, firms that could not afford mainframes worked on a time-share basis; they were, in essence, outsourcing their hosting, disaster recovery, and infrastructure maintenance. During this same period, vendors finally de-coupled hardware and software (that's right, you used to have to buy them in a bundle) and this de-coupling gave rise to software houses to which software development was... outsourced.

One comment that has been repeated to me by clients over the years in regard to IT projects: "We're in [fill in the blank] business, not the IT business." They are expressing their desire to return to core business activities and get out from under the details of information technology maintenance.

An extremely bright Basis specialist I know recently told me that IT directors will not outsource because they are fearful of giving up even a portion of the FTE's who report to them. Clearly, this is so in many cases but such an attitude has more to do with turf protection than with driving value for a firm. As for the consequential argument of "but I can't control outside staff," I would counter with: what do you prefer, controlling a number of individual employees or a vendor contact or two? At any rate, it is outcomes you should be managing, not people.

The final decision fulcrum remains: how far do you want to extend yourself with activities that are not strategic? And what business momentum could you provide your firm with the time freed up?

## Basis is Eternal (and Can Be Done from Anywhere)

Throughout the life-cycle of SAP business applications, Basis support is a necessity. Not everyone is fully aware of what Basis is or what Basis people do, so:

> Definition of Basis (from searchSAP.com): Basis is a set of middleware programs and tools...provides the underlying base (thus the name) that enables applications (such as FI, CO, and SD, for example) to be interoperable and portable across operating systems and database products.

What Basis people do on a regular, um, basis:

- Daily monitoring of system performance
- Data base administration
- Operating Administration

What Basis people do as needed:

- Upgrades
- User administration
- Support packages
- Hardware migrations

As previously noted, Basis support is not necessarily an integral part of the Center of Excellence because it does not directly address business process fulfillment and evolution. However, without solid Basis support, you may well experience unnecessarily long response times, database anomalies, and overly-complex upgrades, all of which will degrade business process fulfillment as well as the nervous systems of most end users.

Basis work is techie stuff so of course we often hear the terms 'Basis Geek', 'Basis Wonk', 'Techno-Weenie', or worse. As it happens, the relative value of a Basis specialist can vary and that variation is often a matter of whether or not an individual is keeping up with the technology.

I am reminded of an internal debate some years ago at META Group in regard to the offshore outsourcing of programming jobs. While one side of the debate argued that America was losing its technical talent, my colleague Stan Lepeak piped up with: "Are we talking about highly talented software engineers or merely hungover Java jockeys spending half the day playing video games before going off at 5:00 p.m. to get liquored up at the VFW?"

The softer point to be made here is that it is unwise to simply grab a "Basis Geek" or two and consider the matter settled. The variation of needs must be matched by a variation of skills, some of which may be required in-house on a full-time basis and others which may best be outsourced.

## Delivery from Anywhere

Vendor distance matters when you're ordering a pizza. It matters much less for Basis support. As in, not at all.

During implementation, project managers love to have a Basis person at hand even when that person is not fully occupied because when they are needed that need is urgent. This urgency is noted by clients who tend to ask how many Basis people they will need on-site after Go-Live. My classic consultant response in years past was "it depends" but in recent years my response has been "very likely zero."

After Go-Live there are fewer urgencies relative to daily Basis administration. Outside of organizations with more than $1B in annual revenues or with very large user populations, few firms really need full-time in-house Basis staff unless they are continually in roll-out mode, or are continually tinkering with software add-ons, or did a very poor job of implementing. I regularly receive requests from clients for "a temporary Basis guy" and the scope of requirements for such requests is a smorgasbord of upgrade assistance, enhancement pack, support for a business intelligence project, and, oh yes, we'd also like some ABAP programming support. In past years, my response was to place a Basis consultant or two for a limited time-frame but inevitably the client was back asking for something more and usually something different which often necessitated sending someone new.

A colleague of mine once claimed "I'm grout" meaning that he was being asked to fill in all the client cracks. Bringing in consultants to serve as "grout" is a normal response except that the consultants do not necessarily need to be on-site.

While a local Basis handyman is, well, *handy,* it may be wiser to outsource most of the following functions, all of which can be done remotely:

*Daily Monitoring:*

- Abnormal system activity

- Poor system performance

- Load distribution across SAP Servers

- Verification of successful backups

- Output Management

- Record Locking administration

- Failed update review

- Notify users of failed jobs

*All Database Administration (Oracle, SQL Server, DB2, etc.):*

- Perform daily monitoring of Database health

- Checking Database logs for abnormal conditions

- Monitoring and projecting Database growth

- Performance and tuning analysis for modifications to the Database structure

*Operating System Administration:*

- Monitoring of operating system errors

- Application of OS patches

- OS tuning and proactive maintenance as required by SAP

Wade Walla is the founder of Group: Basis and has provided remote Basis services for a number of years. When I asked him what is the most frequent comment he gets from clients, he replied, "Relief. They are relieved that they no longer have to carry a beeper around twenty-four hours a day and that they are freed up to do fewer tasks better rather than a multitude of tasks at less than optimum levels."

There is another advantage to outsourcing Basis support, which is to move your organization out of its own technical echo-chamber. As Wade puts it, "If you remain fully internal with one SAP experience and one hardware partner, you will clearly be missing out on the continuous wave of new knowledge, new best practices, and the like."

As an example, when you install SAP, it defaults to a particular format in the installer. If you install the development, QAS and production instances identically (which lesser experienced Basis folks will do), you have missed out on a free and easy disaster recover strategy.

To get out of the Not Invented Here (or, We Do It All Ourselves) you can engage a company that specializes all the time in all aspects of Basis across an array of clients. An advantage in regard to Basis specialists when compared to applications consultants is that Basis work does not require specific business or industry context. Clearly, an incoming applications consultant needs a ramp-up period in order to understand a client's business context. Such a ramp-up is much briefer for a Basis specialist.

Further, many companies have operational environments that are fairly stable. That is the point of buying SAP. Why should firms in this state have to pay full-time salaries to support what is designed to be stable? In other words, why not treat the exceptions as they occur rather than hiring three or four Maytag repairmen?

Another aspect in favor of remote Basis support services is that the Basis workload is much more predictable than is the applications support workload. Even more so than the lag-spike chart presented earlier in this chapter, the Basis workload is a series of lag lag lag with very periodic and predictable spikes. Support packages come around about every three months. You may upgrade every three to four years (and would probably have a need for outside help for this anyway).

But what about the Monday after you've installed a support package? Is Solitaire on tap for your in-house Basis guy? What's happening at the VFW?

Even if you don't go down the line with continuous Basis remote support, you will necessarily need an at-hand life-line for key demand spikes, loss of your in-house resource to illness, retirement or transfer, or if your firm suffers a physical disaster.

While quality and efficacy of enterprise applications consulting and systems integration are incrementally improving, Basis and other SAP technical expertise is growing exponentially. This is most especially evident in the consulting/support environment where Basis specialists are required to keep up their skills to maintain a competitive edge.

In a stable environment, motivating in-house Basis support staff is a challenge. A Basis specialist was once overhead to mutter "maintenance blows." That phrase just about sums up a chronic difficulty clients have in retaining in-house Basis administrators.

## The Cost of Remote Basis Support

Mark Dendinger finds that many clients in small and medium-sized firms (i.e. less than $750M in revenues) either do not know that such services are available or are surprised by how economically viable they can be. "Most clients jump at this offering once they understand the affordability and flexibility."

In a stable SAP environment, Basis work is extremely routine and retaining Basis help is not always easy or even economical. Remote Basis support for the tasks previously listed will cost from $20 to $30 per month per user. Thus if you have 500 users, your monthly cost will be between $10,000 and $15,000. Other cost variables will include the make-up of your applications portfolio (perhaps including non-SAP applications), the version being maintained, and the nature of the user population (e.g. are there a high number of mobile users?).

## Upgrades

The question of whether or not to upgrade, or when to upgrade, and how to upgrade is a matter of constant consternation to SAP managers.

> **To do is to be. Aristotle.**
> **To be is to do. Sartre.**
> **Do be do be do be do. Sinatra.**

In essence, there are three types of SAP upgrade:

*Technical:* in which the focus is to maintain current functionality.

*Functional:* in which system complexity may be reduced and operations streamlined

*Strategic:* in which new and optimized business scenarios are installed as well as a higher version of SAP software.

The most common upgrade is technical/functional.

Many upgrade projects founder due to the classic problem of poor and/or optimistic planning, which often includes using only in-house staff that may have never accomplished an upgrade.

Wade Walla's firm offers fixed fee upgrade services that always begin with a brief but essential upgrade questionnaire that addresses both the current and planned environments. The follow-up to this is an in-depth analysis that addresses key technical aspects but also:

- Is the proposed upgrade steep (e.g. from version 4.2 to ECC 6.0)?

- Is SAP heavily customized and what re-work may be required to upgrade the customizations?

- Is the upgrade accompanied by either the addition of extended applications or a migration/roll-out to other sites?

- Are SAP systems heavily interfaced to other internal business applications?

- Are SAP systems heavily interfaced to external (client/supplier/bank) applications?

The level to which consulting is required is also largely dependent upon a client's internal SAP expertise as well as their past experience. A firm that has already undergone two or more prior upgrades will be better positioned than a firm that has never upgraded.

One often neglected aspect of SAP upgrades is the re-training of end users. I have long observed that the majority of firms tend to spring upgrades on their end user population and provide little or no training. The result is that end users fail to take advantage of new or extended functionality and in many cases, out of fear, will use less of the applications functions than before the upgrade. It is recommended that firms undergoing functional or strategic applications seek outside help to address end user refresher training.

# CHAPTER 5

# Intelligent Business Intelligence

❏ SAP Business Intelligence Matures; Maybe I Can As Well

❏ The Base Architecture of Business Intelligence

❏ Who Generates What, How and Why

# Intelligent Business Intelligence

## SAP Business Intelligence Matures; Maybe I Can As Well

The ability to make business decisions based upon reliable facts that are presented in an actionable format is the grail of responsible business leaders.

Business intelligence (BI) is intended to provide this grail. It embraces data mining, query functions, standard reporting (screen or print), and analytics, all of which can be rolled into a dashboard or "business cockpit."

With a 2008 acquisition of the firm Business Objects, SAP moved into a mature business intelligence environment. Prior to this acquisition, clients were generally stuck with SAP's unwieldy business warehouse and were forced to make do with add-ons such as Cognos (since purchased by IBM) or Crystal reporting, a Business Objects offering.

With Business Objects, a client can benefit from a single platform that brings together data from SAP as well as non-SAP sources and allows for the conversion of that data to business intelligence.

With a fully functioning Business Intelligence, you can:

- Make more informed business decisions
- Be self-reliant since you are no longer dependent on programmers to create new reports.
- Reduce the burden of data collection and reconciliation in favor of analysis.

We will return to the wonders of BI in a moment. But first, my demurral.

I have to admit up front: the subject of reporting has for years made me cringe. It goes back to my days in industry as an IT manager and CIO when it seemed I could not step out of my office into the hallway without hearing: "Where's the listing I asked for?" I could not hold a meeting with a business stakeholder without hearing: "Without this information, I cannot do my job." Since I entered the world of consulting, it has been more of the same, only with greater variation. "If I don't have this information, trucks won't leave the warehouse." "Without that report, we cannot close a sale." And of course the doctor who claimed that "if I don't have this information at my fingertips, patients will die."

Often, the arguments in favor of a report or a query are reasonable. Too often, they represent a fig leaf meant to cover confusion or incompetence.

With SAP, data is more abundant than ever. Much of this data can be information. But information is not intelligence if it is not founded upon business context. Without business context, information serves as fodder in the University of Us by which we can know all the facts of an enterprise but fail to possess the wisdom to turn them into positive action. I make a major argument in the next chapter for Key Performance Indicators as foundations for positive action and true business intelligence can take you much further than KPIs.

End of demurral. Thrive on.

## The Base Architecture of Business Intelligence

The essential order of business is:

1. Gather the core data, either from SAP or non-SAP sources.

2. Integrate the data and assure its coherency and integrity.

   Without Master Data Management (MDM) the task of integrating non-SAP data may be onerous.

3. Organize the data into a usable format within a business framework = business objects

4. Convert the business objects into "intelligence" via chosen vehicle (reports, analytics, dashboards, etc.).

While various other means can be used for steps three and four (Cognos has been a prime option for many SAP clients in the past), Business Objects is now central to the SAP product portfolio.

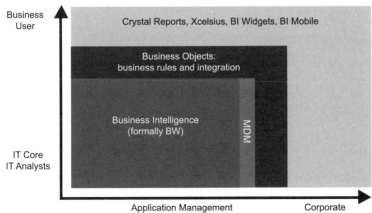

SAP offers a variety of means for expressing the intelligence in its most usable fashion. Crystal Reporting has a long history in the SAP clientele. I have personally used Xcelsius (in a non-SAP environment) over the past four years and can testify to its high level of flexibility and clarity of output as well as powerful, visual what-if capabilities.

The potentially positive note about the current state of SAP business intelligence is best summed up by Joshua Greenbaum (http://ematters.wordpress.com/):

> The bottom line with business analytics is that they typically appeal to the line of business user, and this LOB user is also their primary advocate and buyer. This is a significant departure from both the BI tools and data warehouse side of the market, which have always been more the purview of the IT department, which then parceled out data and reports to the line of business in a now infamous cycle characterized by delays on the part of IT and frustration on the part of the line of business.

This shift of intelligence sourcing from IT to business is a welcome evolution provided said LOB user understands the information received and knows how to leverage it in a positive fashion. Which leads to...

## Who Generates What, How and Why

One final demurral.

In the mid 1980's, when I was the equivalent of what is today a CIO, I decided to take my business stakeholder's constant demand for more information as the highest priority. The solution seemed simple enough as we had recently been given the ability to connect our PCs to the IBM mainframe. Using past reporting requirements as a benchmark, we instituted a daily transfer of key data from the mainframe to various PCs and provided the business stakeholders with query tools by which they could generate the reports they so craved within minutes. This democratic gesture resulted in complete chaos. Sales directors came up with analyses that led them to under price contracts. Manufacturing foremen rescheduled printing jobs based on crappy spreadsheets founded on the wrong data. Spreadsheet reports clashed with the reports coming from our mainframe.

This colossal mistake had many layers but the two most damaging were:

1. the presumption that everyone would understand the nature of information

2. that information, however unreliable, superseded established process.

The business intelligence tools covered herein do not provide business context. That is your task. Further, it is your ongoing duty to constantly frame your business intelligence with context. Without it, your intelligence will simply fuel confusion.

Despite my reservations, I now have a growing sense of confidence that firms are moving ever more in a positive direction in this regard as we now have increased ability to gather coherent data into a form that allows us to rapidly answer complex business questions and increase our productivity and decrease our costs with the answers to those questions.

# CHAPTER 6

# Weathering a Global Financial Crisis: Doing More for Less with SAP

❐ Sitting Tight is Not a Winning Option

❐ Measures of Success

❐ Frankly, Scarlett: Getting Your Business Stakeholders to Give a Damn

❐ The Enterprise Applications Value Chain

❐ Iterative Business Process Improvement – A Sample Exercise

❐ The Daily Doughnut

❐ The Deeper Green: Sustainability

❐ Key Performance Indicators: A Basic List

❐ Three Point Planning

# Weathering a Global Financial Crisis: Doing More for Less with SAP

## Sitting Tight is Not a Winning Option

During the economic downturn of 2000-2003, the market for information technology services simply cratered as client firms went into a collective paralysis.

Spending freeze. Zero budget. Cost and head-count reduction. Belt tightening.

This Hooverian response to that downturn has thus far not been mirrored in the SAP consulting market when it comes to this downturn, especially in the installed base. This time around, with increased maturity, SAP clients exhibit more willingness to make moves toward instance consolidation, process simplification and refinement, and improved user competency. That is not to say that the catchphrase "spend money to make money" has caught fire but at least we have trended away from paralysis.

One welcome development in recent years has been the (mostly) retired notion that SAP is simply IT and that IT is just another utility, like gas or electricity, that can be scaled down to save costs.

Many years ago when I was a CIO, my firm's president issued a blanket order to all departments to reduce costs by 10%. Without his knowledge, I went to work with each of the department heads to determine ways our IT department could help them reduce costs. It was the most productive exercise we had undertaken in my time at the company and the potential net gain was a company-wide cost reduction in excess of 12%. The glitch is that this included a 15% *rise* in the IT budget. This was in 1984 and our president thought as much of IT as he did of the plumbing. My budget was cut by 10% and I left the firm to get into consulting.

Increasingly, client management, both on the business and IT sides, hold the common view that SAP is a business enabler that can be deployed to a) save money and b) increase revenues. How to do both, especially in the wake of the global financial crisis, is the key subject of this chapter.

Bill Wood, a 15 year SAP consultant and SAP project manager who runs R3Now.com says:

> "Many companies are beginning to realize some of the culture transformation promised by ERP. The SAP shops who are realizing the benefits have been live long enough that lower level management and application support are changing from a reactive transaction support mode to more proactive data analysis. This in turn leads to better planning and gives the corporate culture a more strategic orientation. That strategic orientation is leading to value-based spending decisions that are producing real benefits."

What follows is the description of an activity path that should be followed even when the economic weather is fine. One distinction for these economic conditions, however, is a presumption that you will not be adding significant resource or investments; the economic gains that will be realized will be derived from existing resource with a greater focus on value and lesser focus on the daily grind.

There are two key steps to follow in order to weather any fiscal challenge with SAP:

*Step One:* liberate yourselves from non-strategic activities.

*Step Two:* fulfill strategic activities based upon targeted and measurable business benefit.

Even in fairly mature SAP installations, there are countless tasks to be fulfilled on a daily basis that provide little or no value to your enterprise. Many of these tasks are "the things we do because they need doing."

The chart that follows is provided courtesy of Meridian Consulting which helps clients to drive value with SAP.

Note that some process tasks add value in that their completion is a necessity even when the absolute value is low.

Compensating tasks, however, not only do not add value, they suck the oxygen from your support staff as well as the user community. "On average, organizations spend no more than thirty percent

| Customer-Service Tasks | Process Tasks |
|---|---|
| Customer-Serving tasks entail physical, voice, or electronic interface(s) with a customer (i.e. someone who 'consumes' or derives value from your output). Customer-serving tasks begin with words like *respond, serve, reply, delivery, support.* | Process tasks exist solely to mechanically move a process forward. They are usually devoted to creating and managing 'tangibles.' While some process tasks are needed, they do not add value. Process tasks begin with words like *compile, enter, move, stack, store, collate.* |
| Value-Adding Tasks | Compensating Tasks |
| Value-Adding tasks lead up to the customer interface, changing the inputs received so that they demonstrably enhance the quality, utility, or cost competitiveness of the end product or service to the customer. Value-adding tasks begin with words like *transform, enhance, connect, complete.* | Compensating tasks compensate for something not being done right the first time. They do not add value and should be eliminated. Compensating tasks begin with words like *fix, repair, redo, inspect, check, reconcile.* |

of their time on true customer-service or value-adding work," Michael Connor, Meridian's Managing Partner states. "This holds true in firms with mature ERP platforms, which on its surface is surprising." "The problem is twofold," Connor adds. "First, too many organizations fail to adequately automate work, which means lots of time spent on low value 'process' work. And second, the extent to which organizations are willing to devote resources to fixing mistakes is alarming given the lack of reward for such fixes."

As a simple exercise to root out strategic from non-strategic work, ask each FTE in your support group to estimate what percentage of time they dedicate to each of the four activity categories. The result will not be pleasant. Even firms with a fair measure of SAP maturity find that compensating tasks consume at least 25% of their time. Further, such tasks were almost certainly unbudgeted prior to initial Go-Live: fix, repair, redo, inspect, check, and reconcile tasks are the direct result of inadequate response to implementation issues. Further to this point, you may well find that an important measure of these tasks are due to a failure to retire applications that were supposed to be made obsolete when SAP went live or are the result of some short-cut customization or "temporary" work-around. What works around comes around.

Relief from non-strategic tasks may require a "strategic initiative" by which your applications are modified or streamlined. However, one interesting, if nerve-wracking, test is to simply stop fulfilling those tasks in a number of well-chosen areas. Like many of the "issues" that arise in the course of an implementation, a number of the supposed "issues" relative to compensation tasks will simply evaporate.

The measure of strategic or "make work" is more easily illuminated if the enablement domain of a Center of Excellence is in place. Compensating tasks are often shared between IT techies (fix, repair) and end users (re-do, inspect, check, reconcile). In concert, these two groups can weed out tasks that are not driving a business process or assuring data integrity.

## Measures of Success

### Getting Past Total Cost of Ownership

If you haven't measured, for whatever reason, now is the time. I am not referring to the various measures that are only relevant to SAP deployment but to *business* measurement that can be tracked with SAP.

In "SAP Marital Counseling," we pointed out that lack of measurement is an oft-cited post-implementation issue.

| Issue | Long Term Effect | Solution |
|---|---|---|
| There was no quantifiable measurement of business benefits derived from implementation. | Business leadership has not seen "visible" value of SAP investments. | Value Engineering |

In order to weather the current fiscal crisis and to "thrive after Go-Live," measurement is an absolute requirement and it does not have to be a painful experience.

More for less is the goal and the means to that goal are centered upon your ability to measure and your capacity to act. If you are bogged down in the day-to-day operations, that capacity will be limited. If you are not capable of measuring, you will fail.

> "[T]echnology works best when the rules, metrics, criteria, and the means to acquire, process, or analyze information which supports revenue and profitability are understood and defined, " says Bill Wood, using SAP to Improve Revenue and Profitability, R3Now.com online article.

Referring back to the chapter "We Do It Themselves...," you are advised to outsource non-strategic activities in order to gain the capacity to act. As for the measures, we advise simplicity and clarity as opposed to complexity.

The most widely accepted measurement of success for SAP implementations has long been Total Cost of Ownership (TCO). This measurement, favored by SAP software vendors, is rapidly losing relevance due to a combination of a) the rise of value metrics and b) the inherent flaw in TCO itself, namely: it is only half of a viable ROI equation.

Further, TCO usually encompasses only the implementation period and the first two years of operations and thus addresses a software implementation with a life span far shorter than the 15 to 25 years of most SAP installations.

Often, simply technical considerations, such as obsolete IT installations, lead to a reactionary move to replace old applications with SAP. In many cases, client management underestimates the effort required to implement enterprise-wide software. During a lengthy implementation process, the temptation is often to "get it over with" and, in such scenarios, benefits go by the wayside. This is most often the case when the initial vision was cloudy and goals were vague or, as in thousands of cases in the late 1990's, SAP was implemented in a race against Y2K during which benefits could not be addressed simply due to time constraints.

In brief, TCO is a pier and not a bridge.

In this same light, pure financial measures will not suffice. Whether you are looking at Net Present Value (NPV), Return on Investment (ROI), Internal Rate of Return (IRR), or Economic Value Added (EVA), the result will be a) open to multiple interpretations and b) of very little value to the business constituents. Further, results do not provide a diagnostic as to what needs to be changed in order to improve the result. In short, they do not provide enough information about how you are or are not driving value from your SAP investments.

Another red herring associated with some of these measures has been repeatedly cited by clients who refuse to engage consultants in gain-sharing arrangements because they feel that factors other than the work undertaken by consultants may contribute just as much to economic benefit as does the consulting work. (A simple example is a change in economic climate in parallel to a measurement period).

Financial measures do not provide a concrete goal that both business people and IT staff can get their arms around. You cannot use "NPV = $20M or Bust" as your operating slogan.

Finally, such measures do not account whatsoever for intangible benefits. While measuring the value of such benefits can be slippery, they do exist.

The bottom line is that while financial measures should be employed, you will necessarily need something much closer to the business nervous center than such high-level barometers.

## Value of IT Methodologies

There are a variety of proven methodologies for measuring the value of IT. Among them are:

- Total Economic Impact (TEI), a Forrester offering.

- Val IT, provided by the IT Governance Institute

- Business Value Index (BVI), developed and used by Intel

- Applied Information Economics (AIE), developed by Douglas Hubbard of Hubbard Decision Research.

These are all valid methodologies but the implementation of any one of them will require a pretty fair level of IT sophistication and organizational discipline. Further, while the deployment of any of these methodologies will provide more tangible measures than will financial results, they are still focused on the "value of IT" rather than visible, measurable business benefit. I mention them here in order to eliminate them as the driving methodologies for helping you to weather the global fiscal crisis with SAP.

## Frankly, Scarlett: Getting Your Business Stakeholders to Give a Damn

In order for you to succeed in getting visible, measurable business benefit enabled by SAP, your business people will have to give a damn and not just for the duration of a single project.

You will not inspire your business people with generalities about streamlining operations or achieving economies of scale. What is needed is an understandable and relevant target and someone to champion its attainment. Champions are set up to be business heroes.

> "Long ago I learned you merely describe features but you sell benefits. It has to be more than catchy slogans or 'company qualifications,' it must reflect some unique aspect or superiority in a product or service that is meaningful to the intended audience. Entering an SAP project, or re-tooling an existing SAP project with the focus on value and benefit will automatically focus effort and attention on reducing costs and increasing revenue. Define measurable criteria for those results because there is an old business axiom which states 'what gets measured gets done,'" says Bill Wood.

In the introduction, I related the story of a CIO who failed to measure when implementing SAP but later learned how to get business stakeholders to step up. The key was using business language and the glossary was Key Performance Indicators, also known as KPI's. These phrases are the nexus between business and SAP. And if they become your lingua franca, you will surpass business-IT alignment and enter into business-IT dynamism.

Consider the following possibilities:

- Cost of Sales
- Gross Margin

- Gross Profit

- Operating Profit

- Return on Investment

- Return on Sales

- Return on Total Assets

- Yearly Expenditures on R&D as a percent of Net Sales

Clearly, these are some of the prime areas in which most businesses seek to improve.

A business case should address:

1. description of the mission (why it is being undertaken and what is the intended result)

2. project context and priority

3. an assessment of the potential impact on current business for the duration of the project

4. critical success factors

5. anticipated economic benefits and rate of return

6. anticipated strategic benefits and business impact.

Most firms adequately develop the first four elements of a business case, but the latter two points are given bullet point treatment where solid numbers are needed. The intended amount of your financial return and the timeframe in which it will be realized should be decision drivers during your SAP project planning. Thus you will be able to plan to benefit rather than tailoring your plan to time and cost alone. By planning to benefit, you are directly addressing your business stakeholder: we will make you a hero.

## The Enterprise Applications Value Chain

For any enterprise, business results are directly reflected in a Profit and Loss statement. Key Performance Indicators that most directly affect P&L results should be identified as well as the business processes that drive these KPIs.

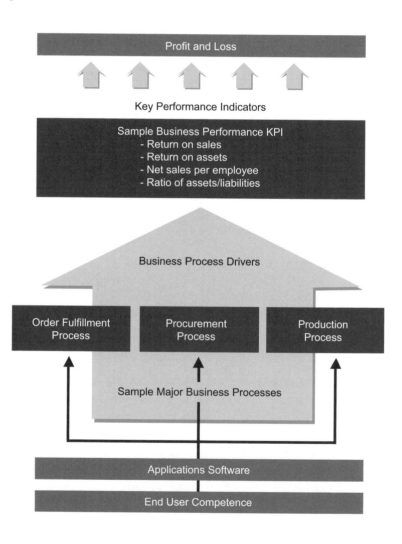

In order to maximize measurable gains:

- determine which performance indicators are the most vital to your firm and which will most clearly reveal benefit or lack thereof;

- accurately measure your current performance in these areas; this can be costly and time-consuming because few firms maintain data that relates to business processes

- determine the current performance measures in your industry sector (average and best performance)

- measure the differences between your current performance and industry averages and bests

- establish a target to be achieved at the KPI level

- identify the business processes that drive KPI results

- improve those business processes with a combination of SAP applications, changes to the process, and assured end user competence.

End users, who have traditionally been trained only to enterprise applications functions, should be trained in regard to their roles in fulfilling business processes and how such fulfillment drives business performance improvement. Many firms fail to receive planned benefits quite simply because the users are not sufficiently competent.

## Iterative Business Process Improvement
## – A Sample Exercise

A prospect once told me that his firm was in a mess and needed more "computerization." When I attempted to re-frame the discussion toward business improvement with the help of computerization, he grew testy. "We're losing five thousand dollars a day and we need to speed things up!" I could not withstand the urge and replied that if we merely sped things up he could lose ten thousand dollars a day.

I don't know if the firm ever got more computerized. I never set foot in the place again.

While much of what follows reveals how SAP "computerization" can enable business process improvement, the core of the exercise is common sense revealed through measurement. Your business process improvements can be incremental or dramatic and the decision as to which tactic to adopt will pivot on the organizational change that is required. Because of organizational complexity, dramatic changes may be more daunting than planned business benefits merited.

In this example, the client is a provider of assemble-to-order goods for which speedy order fulfillment is a major KPI. They have determined that sales order processing is too costly and a drag on order fulfillment turnaround time.

| KPI | Current | Industry Average | Δ | Peer Average | Δ | Target |
|---|---|---|---|---|---|---|
| Cost/Sales Order Processing | $64.00 | $52.00 | ($12.00) | $48.00 | ($16.00) | $40.00 |

| Business process | ERP Models | | Annual Volume | Annual Cost | Target Gain |
|---|---|---|---|---|---|
| Order Fulfillment | Sales, Materials, Management | | 120,000 | $7,680,000 | $2,880,000 |

The client is targeting dramatic reduction in the cost of sales order processing, which, if successful, will yield annual savings of nearly $3M. Of potentially greater benefit is the goal of shortening the order fulfillment turnaround time.

| KPI | Current | Industry Average | Δ | Peer Average | Δ | Target |
|---|---|---|---|---|---|---|
| Order Fulfillment Turnaround | 9.14 | 8 | -1.14 | NA | 7 | - |

It is not necessary to hit these targets in one concerted project. With limited resources, you can effect iterative improvements, each aimed at the same ultimate KPI target.

Measurement begins with the As-Is state for the business process.

| As Is | | | | Step | | | Cumulative | | |
|---|---|---|---|---|---|---|---|---|---|
| Sub-Process | | Task | Time | Lag | Lag % | Cost | Time | Lag | Cost |
| Sales Order Process | 1 | Price, Conditions | | | | | | | |
| | 2 | Accept/Enter Sales Order | | | | | | | |
| | 3 | Order Acknowledgement | 0.040 | 0.040 | 0.4% | $16.00 | 0.040 | 0.040 | $16.00 |
| Purchasing | 4 | Select Vendor | 0.010 | NA | | $4.00 | | | $20.00 |
| | 5 | Approve Purchase | 0.005 | NA | | $2.00 | | | $22.00 |
| | 6 | Prepare Purchase Order | 0.010 | 0.500 | 5.5% | $4.00 | 0.050 | 0.540 | $26.00 |
| | 7 | Received/Stock Materials | 0.030 | 5.000 | 54.7% | $12.00 | 0.080 | 5.540 | $38.00 |
| Production | 8 | Plan Production | 0.020 | 0.200 | 2.2% | $8.00 | 0.100 | 5.740 | $46.00 |
| | 9 | Production | | 1.000 | 10.9% | $0.00 | 0.100 | 6.740 | $46.00 |
| Shipping/ Invoicing | 10 | Packing | 0.015 | 0.300 | 3.3% | $6.00 | 0.115 | 7.040 | $52.00 |
| | 11 | Shipping | 0.020 | 0.100 | 1.1% | $8.00 | 0.135 | 7.140 | $60.00 |
| | 12 | Invoicing | 0.010 | 2.000 | 21.9% | $4.00 | 0.145 | 9.140 | $64.00 |
| | | | | | | | | | |
| Labor = $400 per day | | | Time | Lag | | | | | |
| Total Time and Lag | | | 0.160 | 9.140 | | $64.00 Cost per order | | | |
| Number of Orders per Month | | | 10,000 | | | $640,000 Cost per month | | | |
| Total Workload (Time * Orders) | | | 1,600 Hours per month | | | | | | |

It consists of measuring the human time required for each step in the process as well as the lag time (in days) from step to step. If your process is more time-intensive, lag can be measured in lesser increments. It is usually sufficient to apply a single average labor cost (resource plus overheads) across a process and that is what is done in this example. Note that the $400 per day labor cost includes the average cost of all steps except for production itself. Thus, 10,000 orders per month are being fulfilled in 1.33 hours (16% of an eight-hour working day) with just in excess of nine working days to complete the process.

This business process is deemed important by a client with the following business activity:

Current State/As Is:

- 500 clients, with 65% of all revenues coming from 60 clients
- 500 suppliers with materials purchasing = 60% of all costs.

The various steps in the horizontal process are carried out by diverse vertical departments which is but one of the reasons business process ownership is a key issue.

| Task | Department | Module |
|---|---|---|
| Phone Order | Pre-sales | Sales/Distribution |
| Stock/Delivery Verification | | |
| Accept/Enter order | Sales Order/Processing | Sales/Distribution |
| Order Acknowledgement | | |
| Select Vendor | Purchasing | Materials Management |
| Approve Purchase | | |
| Purchase Materials | | |
| Receive Materials | Warehouse | Materials Management |
| Production | Production/Planning | Production |
| Packing | Warehouse | Materials Management |
| Shipping | | |
| Invoicing and Collection | Accounting | Financials/Sales/Distribution |

In traditional (non-SAP) arenas, each of these departments may have its own separate IT system and interfaces are required to pass orders data from one system to the next. Flow is compromised, as is accountability.

In order to reach our goal of reducing costs from $64 per order to $40 per order and order fulfillment turnaround from nine-plus days to seven days, we will go through three steps although, as will be seen, these could all be accomplished in one go. Many firms founder by trying to do too much too soon, leading to change management issues or too steep a learning curve. In this example we are going to up the stakes with each step.

The first step is a *common sense procedural change* for which no particular information technology is required. (Most clients have

| To Be (A) Common Sense Procedural Change | | | | | | | | | |
|---|---|---|---|---|---|---|---|---|---|
| | | | | Step | | | Cumulative | | |
| Sub-Process | | Task | Time | Lag | Lag % | Cost | Time | Lag | Cost |
| Sales Order Process | 1 | Price, Conditions | | | | | | | |
| | 2 | Accept/Enter Sales Order | | | | | | | |
| | 3 | Order Acknowledgement | 0.040 | 0.040 | 0.6% | $16.00 | 0.040 | 0.040 | $16.00 |
| Purchasing | 4 | Select Vendor | 0.010 | NA | | $4.00 | | | $20.00 |
| | 5 | Approve Purchase | 0.005 | NA | | $2.00 | | | $22.00 |
| | 6 | Prepare Purchase Order | 0.010 | 0.500 | 7.0% | $4.00 | 0.050 | 0.540 | $26.00 |
| | 7 | Received/Stock Materials | 0.030 | 5.000 | 70.0% | $12.00 | 0.080 | 5.540 | $38.00 |
| Production | 8 | Plan Production | 0.020 | 0.200 | 2.8% | $8.00 | 0.100 | 5.740 | $46.00 |
| | 9 | Production | | 1.000 | 14.0% | $0.00 | 0.100 | 6.740 | $46.00 |
| Shipping/ Invoicing | 10 | Packing | 0.015 | 0.300 | 4.2% | $6.00 | 0.115 | 7.040 | $52.00 |
| | 11 | Shipping/Invoicing | 0.020 | 0.100 | 1.4% | $8.00 | 0.135 | 7.140 | $60.00 |
| | 12 | | | | | $0.00 | 0.135 | 7.140 | $60.00 |

| | | | | | |
|---|---|---|---|---|---|
| Labor = $400 per day | Time | Lag | | | |
| Total Time and Lag | 0.150 | 7.140 | | $60.00 Cost per order | |
| Number of Orders per Month | 10,000 | | | $600,000 Cost per month | |
| Total Workload (Time * Orders) | 1,500 Hours per month | | | | |

| | | | |
|---|---|---|---|
| Time Reduction | -0.01 per order | $(4.00) Reduce cost per order | |
| Total Time Reduction | -100 Days per month | $(40,000) Reduced cost per month | |

loads of these). In this example, the client has continued to assign invoicing to accounting, which accounts for the lag between shipping and invoicing. By simply producing invoices at the shipping site, this lag is eliminated and the cost per order processed is slightly shaved.

In a second step, which is *technology-driven,* we take advantage of web-based order entry by which clients no longer call in orders but enter them on the web and assign staff to monitor traffic and occasionally help clients through the process. (While the result would be a major reduction in sales order processing, we assume complete adoption of web order entry in order to simplify this example).

| To Be (B) Technology-Based Procedural Change | | | | | | | | | |
|---|---|---|---|---|---|---|---|---|---|
| | | | | | Step | | | Cumulative | |
| Sub-Process | | Task | Time | Lag | Lag % | Cost | Time | Lag | Cost |
| Sales Order Process | 1 | Monitor Orders | | | | | | | |
| | 2 | Assist Clients | | | | | | | |
| | 3 | Order Acknowledgement | 0.010 | | 0.0% | $4.00 | 0.010 | 0.000 | $4.00 |
| Purchasing | 4 | Select Vendor | 0.010 | NA | | $4.00 | | | $8.00 |
| | 5 | Approve Purchase | 0.005 | NA | | $2.00 | | | $10.00 |
| | 6 | Prepare Purchase Order | 0.010 | 0.500 | 7.0% | $4.00 | 0.020 | 0.500 | $14.00 |
| | 7 | Received/Stock Materials | 0.030 | 5.000 | 70.4% | $12.00 | 0.050 | 5.500 | $26.00 |
| Production | 8 | Plan Production | 0.020 | 0.200 | 2.8% | $8.00 | 0.070 | 5.700 | $34.00 |
| | 9 | Production | | 1.000 | 14.1% | $0.00 | 0.070 | 6.700 | $34.00 |
| Shipping/ Invoicing | 10 | Packing | 0.015 | 0.300 | 4.2% | $6.00 | 0.085 | 7.000 | $40.00 |
| | 11 | Shipping/Invoicing | 0.020 | 0.100 | 1.4% | $8.00 | 0.105 | 7.100 | $48.00 |
| | 12 | | | | | $0.00 | 0.105 | 7.100 | $48.00 |

| | | | |
|---|---|---|---|
| Labor = $400 per day | Time | Lag | |
| Total Time and Lag | 0.120 | 7.100 | $48.00 Cost per order |
| Number of Orders per Month | 10,000 | | $480,000 Cost per month |
| Total Workload (Time * Orders) | 1,200 Hours per month | | |

| | | |
|---|---|---|
| Time Reduction | -0.03 per order | $(12.00) Reduce cost per order |
| Total Time Reduction | -300 Days per month | $(120,000) Reduced cost per month |

The result is fairly minor in terms of reducing lag time (from .04 to .01 days per order) but we have reduced the cost another $12 per order.

The third step is an *SAP-based procedural change* by which SAP-enabled automated purchase processing is implemented. Hereafter, vendor selection and purchase orders are automated. For this example, we have retained the approval process but the net gain is another $8 per order and another half day of lag.

| To Be (C) SAP-Enabled Procedural Change | | | | | | | | |
|---|---|---|---|---|---|---|---|---|
| | | Step | | | | Cumulative | | |
| Sub-Process | Task | Time | Lag | Lag % | Cost | Time | Lag | Cost |
| Sales Order Process | 1  Monitor Orders | | | | | | | |
| | 2  Assist Clients | | | | | | | |
| | 3  Order Acknowledgement | 0.010 | | 0.0% | $4.00 | 0.010 | 0.000 | $4.00 |
| Purchasing | 4  Select Vendor | | NA | | $0.00 | | | $4.00 |
| | 5  Approve Purchase | 0.005 | NA | | $2.00 | | | $6.00 |
| | 6  Prepare Purchase Order | | 0.500 | 0.0% | $0.00 | 0.010 | 0.000 | $6.00 |
| | 7  Received/Stock Materials | 0.030 | 0.200 | 75.8% | $12.00 | 0.040 | 5.000 | $18.00 |
| Production | 8  Plan Production | 0.020 | 1.00 | 3.0% | $8.00 | 0.060 | 5.200 | $26.00 |
| | 9  Production | | 1.000 | 15.2% | $0.00 | 0.060 | 6.200 | $26.00 |
| Shipping/ Invoicing | 10  Packing | 0.015 | 0.300 | 4.5% | $6.00 | 0.075 | 6.500 | $32.00 |
| | 11  Shipping/Invoicing | 0.020 | 0.100 | 1.5% | $8.00 | 0.095 | 6.600 | $40.00 |
| | 12 | | | | $0.00 | 0.095 | 6.600 | $40.00 |

| | Time | Lag | | |
|---|---|---|---|---|
| Labor = $400 per day | Time | Lag | | |
| Total Time and Lag | 0.100 | 6.600 | | $40.00 Cost per order |
| Number of Orders per Month | 10,000 | | | $400,000 Cost per month |
| Total Workload (Time * Orders) | 1,000 Hours per month | | | |

| | | |
|---|---|---|
| Time Reduction | -0.02 per order | $(8.00) Reduce cost per order |
| Total Time Reduction | -200 Days per month | $(80,000) Reduced cost per month |

The three improvements have allowed us to achieve the goals initially set in the KPI exercise of reducing costs to $40 per order… as well reducing the order fulfillment turnaround to less than the goal of seven days.

| KPI | Current | Industry Average | Δ | Peer Average | Δ | Target |
|---|---|---|---|---|---|---|
| Cost/Sales Order Processing | $64.00 | $52.00 | ($12.00) | $48.00 | ($16.00) | $40.00 |

| Business process | ERP Models | | Annual Volume | Annual Cost | Target Gain |
|---|---|---|---|---|---|
| Order Fulfillment | Sales, Materials, Management | | 120,000 | $7,680,000 | $2,880,000 |

| | | To Be | | | C-As-Is | |
|---|---|---|---|---|---|---|
| | As-Is | A | B | C | Gain | Gain % |
| Time Per Order | 0.16 | .015 | .012 | 0.10 | -0.06 | -38% |
| Total Workload | 1,600 | 1,500 | 1,200 | 1,000 | -600 | |
| Cost Per Order | $64 | $60 | $48 | $40 | -$24 | |
| Total Cost Per Month | $640,000 | $600,000 | $480,000 | $400,000 | -$240,000 | |
| Turnaround (working days) | 9.14 | 9.1 | 7.1 | 6.6 | -2.54 | -28% |
| | | | | | | |
| Annual Savings | $(2,880,000) | | | | | |

As for the next iteration of order fulfillment process improvement, note that in our new "As-Is" (To Be C), 90% of the lag is due to the five days awaiting delivery of materials and one day of production.

The logical next step to shortening turnaround time would be an improvement to the materials acquisition process by which we would measure the as-is steps in the same way we did for the order fulfillment process.

This is only one example of what could be dozens of measurable benefits derived from business improvement enabled by sound business process design and SAP business applications software.

While this exercise is simple, the key point is that measurement of key performance indicators should be at the heart of any such effort and that targeted gains must be measured against the costs associated with them.

## The Daily Doughnut

A tale of two doughnut suppliers. With one, I phone in my order before 10:00 p.m. With the other, I enter my order on-line any time before 3:00 a.m.

When I phone in my order, a chatty lady from the doughnut company takes my order and enters it into their sales order system. On occasion, she enters items incorrectly. Oh, well, stuff happens. My new order is added to others and at midnight another lady analyzes the night orders and updates the baking plan accordingly. At 3:00 a.m. when baking begins, someone runs an update to the production schedule that includes my order. At 4:00 a.m. when baking is ended, someone else sifts through the delivery slips and writes up a route order for the delivery trucks. My doughnuts are delivered at 7:01 a.m. and I am asked to pay cash or write a check for them. I am given a receipt that I throw away.

When I enter my order online, the bakery system automatically updates the baking schedule, packing, delivery routing, and cash flow. At 4:00 a.m., my doughnuts are baked during pre-planned batches then are boxed with a pre-printed address label that includes a bar-code for delivery routing. My doughnuts are delivered to my door at 7:00 a.m. where I reflect receipt at the stroke of a light pen. Payment is made automatically. Outside of delivery, my doughnut transaction has required no human intervention and caused zero lags throughout the process.

These are actually the same bakery. The first scenario is before an SAP-enabled transformation.

---

While many information technology expenditures must be made for technical reasons, the costs related to enterprise applications should all be tied to measurable value. We have noted that the most successful firms in this regard are those that value and support their business process owner. In most firms, support for these individuals tends to fade after software is implemented and the result is a predictable return to small and incremental improvements through time, thus eroding the return on investment.

## The Deeper Green: Sustainability

While "green" may connote money, it has come to connote environmental issues all the more. While the greater balance of this book addresses the former, this particular section addresses the latter. They are not mutually exclusive.

Joshua Greenbaum has for some years had the best access to SAP and Oracle senior leadership of any industry analyst. As he wrote in his blog "Enterprise Matters" (http://ematters.wordpress.com/)

> "SAP's customers, according to SAP, produce 1/6 of the world's carbon emissions ... That means that anything SAP can do to support sustainability, efficiency, and other green concepts could have a profound effect on its customers, and therefore a significant quantity of the world's emissions. And, as one of the main goals of SAP's sustainability initiative is to build software solutions that can lower these emissions, and support more efficient and responsible use of other scarce resources like water, enterprise software companies like SAP can indeed become leaders in these efforts."

In the late 1970's I worked on a Control Data mainframe for the City of St. Paul, Minnesota. The mainframe was a few miles away and we had our printouts delivered twice a day. One of my key responsibilities was running demographics data for urban planning with a powerful (at the time) software called Statistical Package for the Social Sciences. Once or twice a week, I would receive a request for a new extract and after entering the parameters I would receive a twenty to thirty page report.

I was only a novice when it came to the full SPSS package and one morning I made the mistake of checking one extra box that provided a third dimension to the report. Early that afternoon the delivery man wheeled in a five foot high printout. This 10,000 page report was obviously unusable for anything other than a bonfire but it was summertime and I was not inclined. The next day I instituted paper recycling for St. Paul's Citywide Data Processing.

Today, such an effort would fall under the heading of "Sustainability." In SAP terminology, sustainability addresses environmental, health, and safety issues. At the risk of getting lost amid a flurry of potential avenues in search of sustainability, I advise that you focus upon core potential within the SAP installed base, namely energy and resource conservation, health and safety, and common sense. Investing in sustainability in these areas is the right thing to do and it should be a given a high priority, not only in altruistic terms but also because *it will improve the health of your enterprise.*

For the moment, sustainability in the context of SAP is a maturing movement. In March of 2009, SAP announced plans to reduce its greenhouse gas emissions down to its year-2000 levels by the year 2020. In support of this initiative as well as client-based initiatives, they named Peter Graf, a longtime SAP honcho, as its first sustainability officer. To date, there is not a lot of detail in regard to "how to" but common sense leads us right back to the starting point of Key Performance Indicators.

Ratio of Recycled Waste to Discarded Waste would have worked for me at the City of St. Paul.

An SAP prospect recently told me that transportation management at his firm consisted of a ball point pen and a notepad. Given that his firm spent $5M a year on transport, it is obvious that basic transport management would save them money (I estimated at least $1.5M). In sustainability terms, it would also have reduced carbon emissions. As KPI's go, we could comfortably settle on Miles per Ton or simply the Cost of Truck Fuel. The firm has other problems since it is in the chicken industry. My prospect could quote the hatch rate, a somewhat crucial KPI for this industry, but he also claimed that safety issues were a great concern, though he did not quote any KPIs in that regard.

My advice is to embed sustainability issues into business process redesign, most especially where the KPIs, like those just mentioned, fairly shout to be addressed. This is not a PR subject unless you have actually done something. If you settle into the standard compliance and reporting elixir offered up by the former Big 4, you may improve compliance and reporting marks without improving the environment at all. However, if you have vastly reduced waste through recycling, reduced carbon emissions through more efficient transport management or manufacturing, or increased plant safety levels, you will have PR gold as well as my admiration.

Below is SAP's sustainability solutions map. SAP applications can enable your firm to address all of these issues.

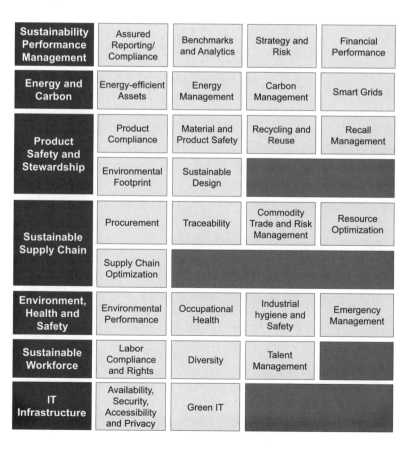

| Sustainability Performance Management | Assured Reporting/ Compliance | Benchmarks and Analytics | Strategy and Risk | Financial Performance |
|---|---|---|---|---|
| **Energy and Carbon** | Energy-efficient Assets | Energy Management | Carbon Management | Smart Grids |
| **Product Safety and Stewardship** | Product Compliance | Material and Product Safety | Recycling and Reuse | Recall Management |
| | Environmental Footprint | Sustainable Design | | |
| **Sustainable Supply Chain** | Procurement | Traceability | Commodity Trade and Risk Management | Resource Optimization |
| | Supply Chain Optimization | | | |
| **Environment, Health and Safety** | Environmental Performance | Occupational Health | Industrial hygiene and Safety | Emergency Management |
| **Sustainable Workforce** | Labor Compliance and Rights | Diversity | Talent Management | |
| **IT Infrastructure** | Availability, Security, Accessibility and Privacy | Green IT | | |

## Key Performance Indicators: A Basic List

### Over-all Performance

Cost of Sales

Current Ratio

Debit Ratio

Gross Margin

Gross Profit

Operating Profit

Return on Investment

Return on Sales

Return on Total Assets

SG&A as a Percent of Revenue

Yearly Expenditures on R&D as a percent of Net Sales

### Planning

Budget Cycle Time

Budget Line Items

Forecast Accuracy

### General Accounting

Cost as a Percent of Revenues

Number Employees to Revenues

Manual Journal Entries per FTE

Number of Bank Accounts Number of Banking Relationships
Period-End Close

Transaction Processing

Transaction Error Rate

Treasury Management Costs

## Procurement

A/P Match Discrepancy

Automated Equipment vs. Batch Transactions

Cost per Purchase Order

Receipt Transaction Processing Time

Dollar Approval Levels

Dollar Value of Purchases per Purchasing Employee

EDI Percent of Total Purchase Dollars

EDI Transaction Percent of Dollars

MRO Order Process Cycle Time

Number of Active Suppliers

Number of Purchases under Long Term Contract

Number of Requisitions

Number of Sources for Critical Material

Number of Suppliers

On-Time Delivery

Percent of Purchases on Procurement Cards

Percent of Purchasing Employees per Total Employment

Percentage of Minority and Women Owned Supplier

## Purchases

Purchase Order Process Cycle Time

Record Integrity (accuracy levels)

Sales per Purchasing Employee

Vendor Delivery Performance Quality (reject rate)

Vendor Delivery Performance Quantity

## Quotations

Average Performance per Salesperson

Average Value of Sales Order

Frequency of Fisits

Lost Order analysis Percent by Reason Code

Order Acceptance Rate

Value of Offered Quotations per Period

## HR and Payroll

Cost as Percent of Revenue

Cost per T&E

Number of Record Changes per Employee

Payroll Errors per Checks Generated

Payroll Transactions per $1B Revenue

Processing Cycle Time

T&E Error Rate

T&E Reports per FTE (per year)

Cost to Process Payroll Checks

## Treasury and Cash Management

Cash Conversion Cycle

Cost of Treasury Management Percent of Revenue

Days Sales in Inventory

FTE Number as Percent of Revenue

Idle Cash Balance Percent of Revenue

Number of Banking Relationships

Working Capital as a Percent of Net Sales

## Accounts Payable

Cost per Invoice

Days Payments Outstanding

Headcount per $500M Revenue

Invoices per FTE

Number of Processed Invoices

Percent of Invoices Processed via Electronic Payments

## Manufacturing

Average Order Batch Size

Capacity Lost to Customer Order Changes

Capacity Utilization per Shift per Work Center

Labor Costs as a Percent of Total Mfg. Costs

Machine Downtime as a Percent of Total Hours

Maintenance Costs as a Percent of Revenue

Material Costs as a Percent of Total Mfg. Costs

Number of Changes to Schedule

Number of Overtime Hours

Number of Rush Orders

Number of Web Breaks Against Roll Usage

Number of Web Breaks per Cycle

Order Receipt to Shipment Cycle Time

Production Costs as a Percent of Revenue

Percent of Newsprint Waste

Schedule Attainment

Set-up Time

Set-up Time as Percent of Order Run Time

Spare Parts Inventory Level in Dollars

Value of Received Orders Press Utilization

## Inventory Management

Days Supply by Part Number

Inventory Accuracy

Inventory Turns (less newsprint)

On Time Delivery of Customer Supplied Material

Percentage of Purchased Material

Slow Moving and Obsolete Percent of Net Sales

Total Dollars of Inventory

Total Dollars of Inventory In-Transit

Total Dollars of SMO Inventory

Velocity

## Accounts Receivable

A/R Cost as a Percent of Revenue

Annual Transaction per A/R Employee

Auto-cash hit rate per invoice

Cash Application per FTE

Bad Debit Percent of Revenue

Days Receivable Outstanding

Processing Cost per Customer Invoice

Processing Cost per Remittance

Receive Beyond 60 Days as Percent of Annual Credit Sales

## Fixed Assets

Fixed Assets Percent of Revenue

Actual Depreciation vs. Planned Depreciation

## Sales

Average Sale per Customer

Cost of Processing a Sales Order

Number of Complaints per Ad

Number of Complaints per Order

Number of Delivery Complaints

Number of New Customers

Number of Partial Shipments

Order Fill Rate by Customer Requested Date

Percentage of Repeat Sales Orders

Returns as a Percent of Sales

Total Dollars of Received Orders vs. Forecast

Total Number of Sales Orders

Total Number of Sales Orders by Product Group

## Sustainability (a very partial list)

Air Quality Index

Reduced Production of Acid-Forming Emissions –

Emission of Greenhouse Gases

Waste Per Production Going to Landfills

Water Consumption to Revenues

Efficiency of Non-renewable Resource Recovery and Use

Proportion of Energy from Fossil and Non-Fossil Fuel Sources

Per Employee Energy Consumption

Job Satisfaction Index – (High rates of job satisfaction are linked to high levels of productivity and creativity).

## Three Point Planning

1. Liberate yourselves from work that adds no value to your enterprise.

2. Measure your performance, target tangible improvement, and realize that improvement through business process reengineering.

3. Embed sustainability in all your efforts.

Thrive after Go-Live.

# CHAPTER 7

# The Care and Nurturing of SAP End Users

❏ Skills Gap; Training Canyon

❏ SAP End User Maturity Model

❏ Begin with the Business Process

❏ Sources and Methods of Continuous Training

❏ Make It So

# The Care and Nurturing of SAP End Users

## Skills Gap; Training Canyon

In 1990, a good friend of mine helped an Australian company go live with SAP R/2. Eight years later, he was called back to the client for new work on SAP R/3. In the course of his project, he spent time with many of the people he had worked with before and in the course of a pub conversation he learned that despite a move from R/2 to R/3 and two subsequent upgrades, the users had received *zero refresher training throughout the eight years*. The effect, they said, was that through time they felt more and more intimidated ('hemmed in") by the applications software and were using less functionality than in previous years. This intimidation only increased with each new change in functionality.

His account of this experience was my first exposure to the neglect of end users in a long-term deployment of applications software. Clients presume that, once-trained, their end user population will self-perpetuate the knowledge base *as if the song remained the same*. But with each change to a business process, each upgrade, each customization, the lyrics change and the user chorus grows ugly.

This is all the more disconcerting because, armed with SAP applications, end users are vastly more empowered than they were with traditional stand-alone applications. With SAP integration, a single cause will have multiple effects. This change increases the volume of user competency or lack thereof.

> "Inadequate training is so much the norm that you wonder whether failure is much more prevalent than we seem to think or if chance has simply made abject failure more rare than it should be," says Joshua Greenbaum.

So as not to leave it to chance, what follows are best practices for achieving a high level of competency and maintaining it through the evolution of your applications platform.

## SAP End User Maturity Model

The following model, like others presented in this book, is derived from the best practices that I have observed since 2001. These practices exceed the simple plane of SAP skills and extend to a more business-oriented dimension.

| SAP End User Maturity Model | | | |
|---|---|---|---|
| Level | Ownership/Drivers | Environment/ Change Management | Expertise |
| 1 Planning | Ownership, authority, and budget for end user training are established within the organization. | End users are prominently included in all change management planning. | Current end user roles and expertise levels are inventoried. |
| 2 Readiness | Training team, methods, and tools have been established. | End Users have received orientation regarding the business goals of SAP adoption and the challenges of an implementation project. | End Users have been identified and new roles and burdens for all are understood. |
| 3 Initial Training | The training team has sufficient time, budget, and material. | End Users have received basic change management regarding roles, expectations, business process principles, and help desk. | End users have received sufficient training to features, functions, roles within business processes, and ongoing governance/help desk |
| 4 Stable Operations | End user competency is being monitored on a regular basis. | Business process changes are communicated to the end user community and workplace adjustments are made where needed. | End users are fulfilling key functions within their business processes and help desk trouble tickets relative to training are at a reasonable level (less than 20%). |
| 5 Expert Plane | A continuous training cycle and budget are established and driven by a recognized entity within the organization. | Portals/interfaces provide users greater visibility and flexibility across applications. | Business process improvements are seamlessly adapted by the end user base. |

If you have already implemented SAP, you may presume that you are already at level 4 considerations. This may be the case for the expertise category but not for ownership/drivers and environment/change management.

It may be onerous to bring in consultants to inventory and rate the skills levels of your individual and collective end user network.

In order to gain an understanding of the current state of your end-user competency, I suggest that you complete a self-inventory regarding each of the best practices included in this model. As for the SAP Maturity Assessment described in an earlier chapter, you should include respondents from a truly representative cross-section of your organization. Ask each respondent to rate your adherence to these practices on a scale of 1 (No Way) to 10 (For Sure) and assess the collective result.

| Level | Ownership/Drivers | Environment/ Change Management | Expertise |
|---|---|---|---|
| 1 Planning | Ownership, authority, and budget for end user training are established within the organization. | End users are prominently included in all change management planning. | Current end user roles and expertise levels are inventoried. |

As previously described, too few firms have established ownership and budget of this subject.

If end users are not included in change management planning, they will be unprepared to adapt to changes resulting from shocks to the application platform.

Whether or not you follow the inventory suggested above, you should have some means of knowing where you stand, both collectively (across the user population) and individually (for each user).

| Level | Ownership/Drivers | Environment/ Change Management | Expertise |
|---|---|---|---|
| 2 Readiness | Training team, methods, and tools have been established. | End Users have received orientation regarding the business goals of SAP adoption and the challenges of an implementation project. | End Users have been identified and new roles and burdens for all are understood. |

Orientation regarding the goals of an implementation project must later extend to the changing goals of SAP deployment. The over-riding goal, of course, is the efficient completion of business processes. Beyond this principle, end users should fully understand their roles in your specific business context. How do they contribute? How can they contribute more? What business benefits are derived or lost depending upon their performance?

In similar fashion, the supervisors of users need to be aware of the roles and burdens demanded of end users. My observation is that such awareness usually exists but is not communicated higher up which leads to an atmosphere in which end users feel neglected.

| Level | Ownership/Drivers | Environment/ Change Management | Expertise |
|---|---|---|---|
| 3 Initial Training | The training team has sufficient time, budget, and material. | End Users have received basic change management regarding roles, expectations, business process principles, and help desk. | End users have received sufficient training to features, functions, roles within business processes, and ongoing governance/help desk. |

As described in the chapter on Centers of Excellence, you should have some entity (internal, external, or both) that is driving continuous training.

Mark Dendinger has considerable experience pitching continuous training to clients and finds that it is a frustrating endeavor. "Most of the clients I've encountered over the years have good intentions but no budget or no champion. Continuous user training is one of those items that never gets high enough on the list of priorities."

End users also need to be aware of what resource is available to them in terms of help desk support, additional training, mentoring and the like.

| Level | Ownership/Drivers | Environment/ Change Management | Expertise |
|---|---|---|---|
| 4 Stable Operations | End user competency is being monitored on a regular basis. | Business process changes are communicated to the end user community and workplace adjustments are made where needed. | End users are fulfilling key functions within their business processes and help desk trouble tickets relative to training are at a reasonable level (less than 20%). |

This is the maturity level that many firms reach after a year or so of SAP deployment and which leads them to fall asleep at the wheel. Two of these important practices can be met simply by monitoring the level of help desk tickets that are relative to training issues. If it is on the rise or already high, you have an obvious diagnostic. Such a solution presumes that you have a professional help desk and sufficient reporting assets to root out training issues.

| Level | Ownership/Drivers | Environment/ Change Management | Expertise |
|---|---|---|---|
| 5 Expert Plane | A continuous training cycle and budget are established and driven by a recognized entity within the organization. | Portals/interfaces provide users greater visibility and flexibility across applications. | Business process improvements are seamlessly adapted by the end user base. |

One additional aspect of the expert plane that may be beyond the realm for most firms is the measurement of end users in regard to business process fulfillment. This would entail an identification of individual users involved in a given process and a means of monitoring the fulfillment of process steps. One of the burning questions posed to me regularly is: how do we motivate our end users to improve their competency? One way would be to institute end user monitoring in such a fashion and to compensate end users with exceptional performance.

Once you have a handle on the level of competency of each individual user, you should be able to act appropriately to raise that level incrementally.

| User Level | Attributes | Needs |
|---|---|---|
| Super User | An expert who also a) provides guidance to other end users and or b) makes useful recommendations for business process improvements. | A raise |
| Expert | Can fulfill all required tasks as well as crucial trouble-shooting. Accelerates the business process. | Recognition |
| Garden Variety User | Can fulfill all required tasks and some level of troubleshooting. | Mentoring |
| Medium Rent | Can fulfill most tasks but does not step beyond known boundaries to learn more (e.g. reporting, exceptions handling, trouble-shooting). | Mentoring and more training |
| High Rent | Can fulfill basic tasks but requires help for anything "out of the ordinary." | More training (mentoring won't help) |

## Begin with the Business Process

Consider the following true story emanating from a firm that claimed its SAP user base was "world class."

Alice (name changed) was their senior SAP-trained sales order processing specialist. According to the SAP sales order configuration, any order directly entered by a salesperson under $10,000 was automatically passed from sales to manufacturing and distribution, thus streamlining the orders-to-cash process. Alice was responsible for review of all orders over $10,000.

Since large orders are the life-blood of any firm, it may be presumed that Alice would check these orders the instant they came in. Upon review, we first found a possible design flaw in that Alice received no special prompting that such an order was in the queue. This would not have been a problem except that Alice did not check her incoming sales screen on a regular basis. Instead, she waited until the end of a working day to review and approve *the largest orders her company had received that day.*

Thus, Alice had fulfilled the business process to the letter while holding up untold sales orders and adding up to one full day to the orders-to-cash business process. Because she was trained to the *functions* of sales order monitoring and not to her role in the all-important *process.*

While you might think that Alice should have quite naturally been aware of this glitch, it should be noted that none of her co-workers, including her immediate supervisor, ever reviewed her role with her. The firm that claimed that its user base was "world class" was actually "run-of-the-mill" with a collection of users who knew the features and functions but were clueless about the relative business processes. Should the design have included a prompt when a large order was awaiting review? Perhaps. But no prompt is needed if the user knows the business process. The elimination of such "prompt" or "alert" requirements is one excellent example of the virtues of teaching the business process to users.

In fulfilling continuous end user training, each step should begin with a review of the business processes before moving on to functions and reporting. All subsequent training will be propelled by this essential context.

New employees without ERP experience tend to compare SAP to outgoing legacy systems and note that they will now have more screens to address, more data to enter, and more transactions to fulfill than before. The first natural result is resistance. This resistance will be largely eliminated if the users understand how they are now using "integrated enterprise software" and that many other tasks related to the legacy organization will now be eliminated.

Business process orientation will necessarily add one half day to initial end-user training but users will be primed to avoid the "click here/click there" utilization ruts and their progress toward the expert plane will be accelerated.

## Sources and Methods of Continuous Training

The firms that provide formal continuous education tend to rely on a single source from amongst super users, the applications support team, and outside sources.

| Method | Advantage | Disadvantage |
|---|---|---|
| Super User | The user group takes responsibility for making it all work. | Hard to ID a super user; super users do not always know the answer to 'why?' |
| Applications Team | Can answer the question 'why?' | Not empathetic to user group concerns. |
| Outsource | Training specialists are on the scene. | Lack of client context. |

Provided that end users have received business process orientation, the nettlesome question of "why" should be largely eliminated. (Why do I have five screens for that function when I used to have only two? Why do I have to validate this function? Why would I do this before I do that?)

In such a case, super users or outside trainers may well be the most strategic and cost-effective choice, thus liberating the applications team to focus on improving the business processes.

This leads us to the notion of role-based training as users have become increasingly unique. Back when SAP introduced portals, I found myself with an early adopter who was walking me through a functional problem while moving across a variety of applications. At one point I asked, "Are we in SAP now?" His reply: "I never know exactly when I'm in SAP."

In this light, the method or methods deployed are even more important than the source of continuous training as role-based training cannot be entirely provided to all users. It is now incumbent on users to educate themselves.

**Mentoring:** This method can best be performed with a super-user approach by which super users mentor individual users. When combined with any of the other training methods, it assures both personalization and an environment of relevant business context.

**Instructor-led:** An important part of a blended approach, instructor-led training will never be completely replaced by technology because no technology publicly available has been able to replicate the benefits of face-to-face interaction, particularly in the areas of soft skills. My preferred scenario is for super users to regularly provide a "skills uplift" session for small groups of users and on an annual basis to have more general sessions led by an outside instructor capable of bringing best practices to your enterprise.

**Computer-based training/CD-ROM:** CD-ROM delivery is convenient, scalable, and bandwidth-friendly. However, this source of training is generic, cannot be related to specific business processes at your firm, and can quickly become outdated. I do not advise inclusion of this method in your mix.

**Online:** There are a variety of online offerings. The most widely used packages are offered by RWD Technologies. When choosing among the various vendors, selection criteria should include a) simulation capability so that the training content will be in your firm's context, b) tracking/scoring capacity, and c) self-pacing/bookmarking capability.

**E-learning delivery platforms:** These are an extension of basic online training offerings that can categorized into three types according to business application: asynchronous classrooms, synchronous classrooms, and electronic performance support systems (EPSS). Products in this category enable the design, delivery, and tracking of Web-based training courses on a small scale, and require little IT involvement to install and run. Full-scale e-learning platforms are probably beyond the reach or requirements of firms with less than 500 end users.

The very worst method of continuous training is having outgoing employees train their replacements. Think about it. Often, one or neither is available for such handover. There is also this situation: "Delores, I want you out of here at the end of the week. Oh, and before you go, be sure that Larry knows everything you know about SAP."

Training can be boring, no doubt about it. Some of the training programs I've seen through the years have interesting features but the delivery is clumsy, humorless, and stultifying. If this, then that. Go back to step 4. Try again.

What we need is a way to train users by which they will be both motivated and not bored. I leave the former challenge to you (internal certification program with incentives?) and the latter challenge to the training firms.

## Make It So

It is well-established that people have preferences in regard to training methods. A vibrant competency program will motivate users to improve their skills and provide a variety of means to do so.

Without a confident and well-versed end user population, you will see your benefits go out the back door.

As detailed earlier, ownership and budget of this activity is hard to pin down. It will be less difficult if you have a business-centric organization (like the Center of Excellence) wherein ownership and budget would be invested in either the business process owner or each of the related lines of business.

Here again is how measurable value is driven. Note that the anchor to this process is the end user. If you are in earnest about driving business value, you have to invest in that anchor. Continuously.

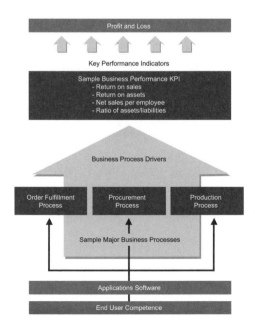

CHAPTER 8

# From Supplier to Advisor:
# A New Chair for SAP

❒ SAP Life After Functionality

❒ News Flash: SAP is not a Not for Profit

❒ Working Toward Partnership with Tiered Maintenance Costs

❒ Drive at Your Own Pace (and Show SAP Where You're Going)

# From Supplier to Advisor:
# A New Chair for SAP

## SAP Life After Functionality

If for no other reason than sunk cost, very few clients ever switch out from SAP for something else. As such, SAP clientele is a captive audience. Before you license SAP software, you are pursued. Once you license, you have become "acquired."

Back in the mid 1990's, that sense of acquisition wasn't there. Firms installing SAP continued to be courted because of the urgent need for client references and testimonials. (When I started working in the world of SAP in 1995, U.S. prospects were asking to talk to firms that had SAP already installed. Nearly none could be referenced).

To improve the client acquisition process, SAP created SAP Consulting in 1997 so as to no longer merely be, in their words, "cheering from the sidelines," and thus took a greater direct stake in client implementation success.

By 2001, however, the SAP client base had grown quite large and from this time forward clients have largely felt captive. For years, they were offered upgrades, most of them relative to enhanced functionality, at a pace that was too frequent and presented in fairly magisterial terms. "You will upgrade by this date or we will cancel your support."

Since about 2003, when SAP new license sales began to take off after a four year lull, there has been a growing sense of neglect among installed base clients. First, there was a great hullabaloo about the revolution of NetWeaver but the clientele largely shrugged. Since losing the author of NetWeaver, Shai Agassi, in 2006, SAP is talking much less about NetWeaver. At the 2006 North American SAPPHIRE, SAP announced an end to upgrades based upon increased business functionality. While this announcement did relieve those clients with upgrade fatigue, it also clearly suggests that now SAP can "do it all," which of course it cannot.

More recent "new horizons" for SAP have been in the small to medium enterprise market with Business One and a first stab as Software as a Service (SaaS) known as Business ByDesign. No, that is not a typo: SAP has coined a new term ByDesign. This offering is targeted at relatively small clients and is not directly relevant to readers of this book.

More recently, SAP has announced its intention to raise maintenance fees from a longstanding 17% to 22% and has done a very poor job of explaining to its clientele just why this is a good thing. After a brief hiatus as a recognized SAP industry analyst, I was quickly back on the map with a simple blog post entitled "SAP: Stop Chopping off the Tallest Heads to Make Everyone Equal."

More to follow on this subject given that a 30% hike in maintenance fees is not a trivial matter.

## News Flash: SAP is not a Not for Profit

SAP of course repeats the mantra about being in partnership with its clients. Whenever any vendor raises this hoary claim, I cannot help but cringe because the elements of partnership (mutual interest, mutual financial incentives) seldom exist. (Too many systems integrators even go so far as telling you that they should be your 'trusted advisor' even while they are charging you fixed-fee rates).

While SAP can, in large part, become something of a partner, the foundational fact is that they are a software supplier to whom you paid money for the licenses and continue to pay for support of those licenses. Maintenance revenue is the recurring fee lifeblood of any applications software firm and SAP is no exception.

Here, with Euros converted to dollars, are SAP's 2008 high level results:

| Overall SAP Results (2008) | |
|---|---|
| Revenue | $15.39 |
| Cost | -$11.80 |
| Operating Profit | $3.59 |
| Operating Margin | 23% |

| Overall SAP Support Results (2008) | |
|---|---|
| Support Revenue | $6.12 |
| Software and Software Related Services | -$2.31 |
| Operating Profit | $3.80 |
| Operating Margin | 62% |

I have been tracking SAP financials since 1995 and these are fairly typical results. Further, they are based upon a 17% annual maintenance rate, so one can easily extrapolate what 22% would have yielded.

A rate hike for maintenance, accompanied by very little in the way of justification, is only one issue that can degrade the notion of partnership. The other is a persistent presumption that they know what's best for you at every turn.

What infuriates installed base clients is the behavior of SAP after licensing. Too often, SAP is like a car dealership with a salesman who not only sells you the car but also sits in the passenger seat and before you have left the lot *is telling you to buy next year's model.* Then SAP proper tells you how to drive the car while also nagging you to change the oil, inflate the tires, and speed up before the light changes. Most clients agree that SAP software performs well, is rich in functionality, provides impressive integration features, and can be adapted to changing business environments. These same clients grow annoyed when SAP tells them how to get the most out of the software no matter what their business context.

Right or wrong, some clients do not want to upgrade every third year or so and are quite content to run what they have in a way they see fit. But in years past, a failure to upgrade according to SAP's timetable has led to threats, or realities, of a lack of version support.

Right or wrong, some clients do not want to retro-fit Solution Manager.

Right or wrong, some clients do not want to extend their applications footprint or add a business intelligence layer.

Right or wrong, some clients want to simply shake out their SAP plants and consolidate their gains before moving onward.

Right or wrong, these clients have been paying 17% annual maintenance fees and will soon be paying 22%.

Admittedly, with over 50,000 clients as well as hundreds of industry and financial analysts and hundreds more technical and services partners, SAP is not lacking for advice. All the same, my advice to them in the realm of "partnering" with a captive installed base is to:

1. buck up their once-impressive levels of R&D

2. provide an equitable maintenance arrangement

3. stop assuming that you know what's best for the client when it comes to software deployment.

In fairness, SAP has cultivated a rich eco-system including The SAP User Group Executive Network (SUGEN), which comprises all 31 active user groups around the world, mentoring networks (e.g. the aforementioned BPX program), and a wealth of web-based thought leadership. My beef is not what they do globally for its collective client base; it is what they do with individual clients.

## Working Toward Partnership with Tiered Maintenance Costs

Back when mySAP first came out, there was a lot of confusion amongst R/3 clients regarding what it would take to move over to the new platform. The basic policy of SAP was that it required new licensing rather than simply an upgrade. What actually occurred was a furious round of negotiation with results falling between these two poles:

*Low end:* complete re-licensing with no credit for prior years of SAP licensing and maintenance

*High end:* discounted re-licensing based on credit for prior years of SAP licensing and maintenance.

I have worked with clients who have more than 250 instances of SAP as well as clients who customized the software into oblivion. Such firms tend to suck SAP support resources on a continuous basis.

I have also worked with clients who possess a single instance and a single data center as well as a savvy end user population. Calls to SAP by such firms are not a burden.

Under the new regime, both clients will inevitably be paying the same rate of maintenance.

If your firm is a screaming mess, you should be paying a high end maintenance fee. SAP deserves it. But if your consumption of SAP time and intellect is only marginal, you should be paying less.

The negotiations precedence regarding mySAP should be carried forward regarding maintenance fees. If you feel your firm is a good SAP citizen and you can back that up with evidence of a) low to mid-level consumption of SAP support services and/or b) internal investments for your own SAP support, you will have an excellent foundation.

In regard to your consumption of SAP support services, all the stats are already there. Number of calls, issues, resolution time, etc. In regard to your internal investments there are probably more than you may have considered:

- Outsourced help desk – reduces the volume of annoyance calls to SAP through improved routing and service

- High level or outsourced Basis administration – idem

- Internal Center of Excellence with a strong focus on user competency and robust functionality

- High level of participation in ASUG or ASUG-like client-to-client support and sharing of best practices and/or participation in the SAP Community Network (SCN)

- Full compliance with SAP upgrade policy (it is obvious that a 4.7 client is more of a burden than a 6.0 client)

None of this is *absolutely* measurable but remember that as an acquired client with a probability of 15 to 20 years as such, you do not have to simply write a check and sigh. Already, SAP is conceding that the lift from 17% to 22% will be progressive and there are further indications that it will not be an absolute. If you are considering licensing more software from SAP, you have even more room for negotiation.

I would also advise that you dial the negotiation to at least one level above your day-to-day SAP sales rep. Their revolving door, especially for small and mid-market clients, creates a breezeway that does not contribute to fruitful partnership. I know one CIO in the mid-market who no longer even takes a proffered business card when he meets his new SAP account executive. "My Outlook is already littered with names of the departed."

If you are using SAP Consulting for any services, you should have another bargaining chip, but there are caveats in this regard.

First of all, SAP Consulting chronically has the highest hourly fee rate in its domain. Yes, higher than Accenture, higher than IBM, higher than Deloitte. More important, however, is the difficulty in bundling SAP consulting into the software or support mix. SAP seems to believe that if an SAP software salesman and an SAP services salesman are ever in the same room, the universe will explode. All the same, if you are negotiating a license for more SAP applications and are considering SAP Consulting as your implementation partner for those applications, the consulting costs should be part of the negotiation equation (either in favor of licensing discounts or fee discounts). Insist upon it.

---

Footnote: Forrester provides a Software Licensee's Bill of Rights, driven primarily by the long-time industry analyst Ray Wang. Needless to say, none of the enterprise software suppliers, including SAP, publicly recognize this document or its precepts. While this 17 page document isn't free, it may well be worth the modest investment to obtain it.

## Drive at Your Own Pace
## (and Show SAP Where You're Going)

I once had a client that continually bought my team's services in increments. First we completed a small project that improved logistics reporting across multiple sites. Then we fixed some terrible sales order processing software that had been written by a dubious Norwegian firm. We were subsequently asked to extend our services to more of their country offices. After about a year of this, I proposed to the client that we establish an IT strategy in order to more efficiently advance their evolution. What sunk this boat was my firm's request that we be given foundational insight into the client's company strategy. "We will never share our strategy with outsiders!"

While this response was somewhat draconian, it served as a reminder of the true context of business software; namely, that it is an enabler and business leaders are the enabled.

It is a fact that you are not now using SAP the way they want you to nor will you ever use SAP the way they want you to. Keep the SAP cart behind your business horse. Stick to your strategic guns. Enter your own tired metaphor here.

You can get ahead of the SAP sales curve by involving them in your strategic roadmap. Trust that they will pull out their own roadmaps (they have hundreds) but these will divert you into the software subject. Unless your strategy already addresses software, firmly decline and get back to your own plans.

The key is to approach SAP beyond the level of the sales rep. One of SAP's evident strengths is its support eco-system which begins at SAP itself and extends to services and technical partners. Where they can increasingly provide help is around your applications architecture (operating system, data base, master data management, integration with non-SAP applications, and all other aspects of the big technology tent known as NetWeaver). Other subjects such as value engineering, sustainability, and GRC (Governance, Risk, and Compliance) are currently in the SAP wheelhouse and all merit your attention. Since SAP's acquisition of Business Objects (Bob J to insiders), the organization has committed time, money, and resource into leveraging new business intelligence assets to the benefit of the installed base.

In brief, turn SAP into one of your advisors which will serve not only to dampen the sales flame but also to put them into your context where their advice will be more effective.

## Last Word Freak

In the course of a seminar, I was once posed one of those "can you put it all in a nutshell?" questions. What single piece of advice could I give to a firm that would "wrap it all up in a bow"?

My answer: be obsessed about business processes.

Everything else described in this book flows from that frame of mind. Business process improvement yields measurable business benefit. SAP assets support continuous business improvement. End users drive business processes with the help of those assets. The effects of business process improvements (or declines) are directly reflected in a Profit and Loss. Business process enablement and streamlining is the core reason why you have SAP. If it wasn't before you read this book, I trust that it will become so.

# Sources

A book's worth of advisory should never be based merely on an author's "experience" and "insight." While it is evident that much of this book is derived from my own background as an SAP consultant and industry analyst, I continue to be educated by a collection of friends and colleagues as well as readers of The New SAP Blue Book.

As such, the contents of this book are largely the result of "collective insight."

## Research

While at META Group (now folded into Gartner Inc.) and Performance Monitor from 2001 to mid 2007, I had the pleasure of satisfying my curiosities regarding what does and does not work in the realm of SAP/ERP. Over a six and half year period, I led or participated in a variety of studies supported by deep client input, including (at META Group):

| Subject | Respondents | Year |
|---|---|---|
| ERP Installed Base | 466 | 2002 |
| The State of ERP Services | 437 | 2003 |
| The State of CRM Services | 355 | 2002 |
| The State of CRM Services | 263 | 2004 |
| Applications Management Services | 315 | 2003 |
| ERP End User Competency | 142 | 2003 |

From mid-2005 to mid-2007, working in my own firm, I upped the ante in regard to both data quality (through improved filtering) and quantity.

| Subject | Respondents | Year |
|---|---|---|
| SAP Systems Integrators | 693 | 2005 |
| Oracle Systems Integrators | 645 | 2005 |
| People Soft Systems integrators | 666 | 2005 |
| SAP Systems Integrators | 809 | 2007 |
| Oracle Systems integrators | 864 | 2007 |
| CRM Systems Integrators | 709 | 2006 |
| Application outsourcing Firms | 709 | 2006 |
| Application Development and Maintenance Firms | 864 | 2006 |

While the latter studies were focused on the field performance of service providers, there was a considerable amount of input regarding goal attainment, issues and resolutions, implementation or deployment best and worst practices, and "data narratives" that describe client/respondent priority shifts after Go-Live.

Among the most striking lessons learned across these studies (in no particular order):

1. *You Get How You Pay For:* fixed-fee implementation projects are the least successful; value-based fee projects are the most successful (if you can measure).

2. *Desperately Seeking…:* The number one reason clients opt to outsource SAP applications support is the desire to obtain hard-to-find SAP skills.

3. *Tell Me If You've Heard This One Before:* The large systems integrators tend to perform fairly well in the Fortune 500 market and very poorly in all other markets.

4. *Latch-Key Kids:* End users can't get their parents' attention.

5. *I Said I Wanted Chicken But Now I Want Steak and Later I Will Be Happy to Have a Hot Dog:* The client group mindset changes radically between the time they choose a systems integrator and the time they start a project. Then nearly everything changes again after go-live. (Moral: it is good to

have an articulated long-term vision before starting down the
SAP path).

6. *My Last Confession Was During Business Blueprint (The
   Privacy of the Confessional):* in public settings, clients blame
   SAP or their systems integrator for project issues. When
   provided an anonymous platform, they place far greater
   blame on themselves.

7. *A Day at the Dentist:* measurement of business performance
   is deemed (incorrectly) as painful as root canal.

Across the years, clients are making progress but only incrementally
as opposed to leaps and bounds. Since 2002, clients have become
more SAP self-reliant and less dependent upon systems integrators
(after Go-Live). More clients are adopting a long-term approach
to SAP evolution and fewer clients are mangling their applications
with unnecessary customizations.

## Blogs and Websites

There are a number of SAP-sponsored blogs. You can best find
them listed with a simple Google of "SAP blogs." As in all things
SAP, these blogs tend relate to software and technology issues rather
business and organization issues.

Blogs are not necessarily permanent and, being a fitful blogger
myself (http://sapsearchlight.blogspot.com/), I know that they are
not always regularly updated and are prone to being moved. All
the same, these are blogs that I find very useful and thus follow
regularly:

http://sapmesideways.blogspot.com/ The ongoing, anonymous
"log" of a troubled SAP implementation project by a project
member. Fly on the wall, real-life insight.

http://ematters.wordpress.com/ This excellent blog by Joshua
Greenbaum includes coverage that extends beyond the SAP/

Oracle horizon. SAP clients receive a reliable viewpoint on the SAP forward horizon.

http://blogs.zdnet.com/Howlett/ Dennis is the Hunter S. Thompson of IT bloggers. He regularly holds SAP feet to the fire.

http://blog.softwareinsider.org/ Ray Wang often writes customer-centric calls to action and provides regular and invaluable tips.

http://fscavo.blogspot.com/ Frank Scavo is a clear-minded observer of client best practices and is skilled at putting the spotlight on dubious vendor assertions.

www.jonerp.com If you are an SAP consultant of any stripe, this site should be on your daily checklist.

www.r3now.com This is Bill Wood's treasure trove of information and articles emanating from fifteen years of field experience.

# About the Author

Michael Doane has thirty-five years of business and information systems experience, including twelve year of industry, sixteen years in enterprise applications consulting, and six years as an industry analyst.

In addition to prior roles as an SAP practice lead at Grant Thornton and The Consulting Alliance, Mr. Doane has directed several major consulting engagements for large systems integrators, most notably in financials and logistics, in North America, Europe, and Asia. Prior to entering the world of consulting, he was the European IS director for the Plessey Company Ltd. and for Ferry Peter, a division of Wiggins Teape.

He has been publishing information about SAP since 1996. In addition to this book, he is the author of *The SAP Blue Book, a Concise Business Guide to the World of SAP* and co-author, with Jon Reed, of *The SAP Consultant Handbook.*

Since 2001, he has been advising clients on strategies, implementation and integration strategies, service provider selection and management, and best practices and methods for deriving value from enterprise applications investments.

# Contributors

Michael Connor is founder and CEO of Meridian Consulting (www. meridian-us.com) and a significant contributor to The New SAP Blue Book. We have been sharing intelligence and collaborating with clients since 1997.

Jon Reed has been advising clients and consultants for more than fifteen years and is now the recognized leader in the field of SAP career guidance. We have been working together in the SAP fields since 1995. His website is www.jonerp.com

Joshua Greenbaum is an independent industry analyst who writes for SAP publications and is a valued advisor to upper management at SAP, Oracle, and other enterprise applications software firms. His website is http://ematters.wordpress.com/

Mark Dendinger has led a number of successful SAP systems integration firms since 1995 and has extensive contacts with SAP America and a vast network of SAP consultants.

Kay Tailor is an accomplished SAP architect/technician who has been active in the SAP fields since the mid 1990's.

Wade Walla is the founder of Group: Basis and has a considerable ability to demystify "the technical."

Dane Anderson has worked as an IT outsourcing provider and since 2003 has been a prominent industry analyst covering the IT services and outsourcing marketplace.

John Ziegler was one of the first group of non-European consultants at SAP America. He has managed dozens of SAP projects since 1992.

Bill Wood has spent fifteen years helping clients go live with SAP. His website is www.r3now.com

# Ordering Information

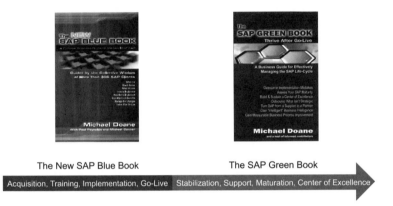

The New SAP Blue Book       The SAP Green Book

Acquisition, Training, Implementation, Go-Live    Stabilization, Support, Maturation, Center of Excellence

## These books are not available in bookstores.

**Direct order:**

Send an e-mail to michael@michaeldoane.com providing:

- Your Name
- Business Name (optional)
- Your purchase order number (if applicable)
- Delivery Address
- Invoice Address (if other than delivery address)
- Delivery Method (Standard mail, Fedex, other)
- Quantity Ordered
- Phone (for assured delivery)

You will be billed when books are delivered.

**Order Online:**

Go to www.michaeldoane.com